Instructions to the Cook

INSTRUCTIONS
TO THE COOK

A Zen Master's Lessons in
Living a Life That Matters

BERNARD GLASSMAN
& RICK FIELDS

BELL TOWER ° NEW YORK

Published by Bell Tower, an imprint of Harmony Books, a
division of Crown Publishers, Inc., 201 East 50th Street,
New York, New York 10022. Member of the Crown
Publishing Group.

Random House, Inc. New York, Toronto, London, Sydney,
Auckland

Harmony, Bell Tower, and colophon are trademarks of
Crown Publishers, Inc.

Printed in the United States of America

Design by Barbara Balch

Library of Congress Cataloging-in-Publication Data

Glassman, Bernard (Bernard, Tetsugen)
        Instructions to the cook : A Zen master's lessons in
    living a life that matters / Bernard Glassman and Rick
    Fields.
            p.   cm.
        1. Religious life—Zen Buddhism.   2. Cookery—
    Religious aspects—
    Zen Buddhism.   3. Bakers and bakeries.   I. Fields, Rick
    II. Title.
    BQ9286.2.G57   1996
    294.3'444—dc20   96-5153
                                                            CIP

ISBN 0-517-70377-7

10 9 8 7 6 5 4 3 2 1

I dedicate this book to my teacher, Hakuyu Taizan Maezumi Roshi, who died on May 14, 1995, at the early age of 64. Maezumi Roshi was the father of our family lineage in this country and Europe and a master Zen chef. I wish to offer him the following vows:

> Playing freely in self-fulfilling and
>   other-fulfilling samadhi,
> I vow to maintain and nourish
>   the One Buddha Mind Seal.
> Life after life, birth after birth,
>   practicing diligently,
> I vow to never let die the wisdom seed
>   of the buddhas and ancestors.
> Truly! I vow this to you.
> In deep gratitude,

Bernard Tetsugen Glassman

A deep bow to all the inhabitants of the Greyston Mandala, especially the pioneering residents of 68 Warburton, the staff of the Greyston Bakery, and the members of the Zen Community of New York, for their courage and dedication to working with the rejected parts of society and self in all the ten directions.

Our deepest acknowledgment is to Zen Master Dogen and his *Tenzo Kyokun (Instructions for the Zen Cook)*, which inspired us. The translation we have referred to appears in *From a Zen Kitchen: Refining Your Life*, by Zen Master Dogen and Kosho Uchiyama, translated by Thomas Wright (John Weatherhill, New York and Tokyo, 1983).

Instructions to the Cook

When I first began to study Zen, my teacher gave me a *koan*, a Zen question, to answer: "How do you go further from the top of a hundred-foot pole?"

You can't use your rational mind to answer this *koan*—or any Zen question—in a logical way.

You might meditate a long time and come back to the Zen master and say, "The answer is to live fully."

That's a good beginning. But it's only the rational, logical part of the answer. You have to go further. You have to demonstrate the answer. You have to embody the answer. You have to show the Zen master how you live fully in the moment. You have to manifest the answer in your life—in your everyday relationships, in the marketplace, at work, as well as in the temple or meditation hall.

When we live our life fully, our life becomes what Zen Buddhists call "the supreme meal."

We make this supreme meal by using the ingredients at hand to make the best meal possible, and then by offering it.

This book is about how to cook the supreme meal of your life.

This book is about how to step off the hundred-foot pole.

This book is about how to live fully in the marketplace.

And in every other sphere of your life.

Most people come to see me in my capacity as a Zen teacher because they feel that something is missing in their lives. You might even say that most people come to Zen because they are hungry in some way.

Maybe they are successful in business but feel that they have neglected the deeper, more "spiritual" aspects of life. These people come to Zen to find meaning. Other people have devoted so much time to their own spiritual search that they end up having neglected their livelihoods. These people come to Zen to "get their life together."

Then there are people who want to practice Zen for health reasons. They find the posture and breathing that accompany Zen meditation especially helpful. The regular practice of Zen meditation, for example, lowers blood pressure and improves circulation. The lungs function better, so that you can breathe more deeply and powerfully.

Other people are drawn to Zen for "self-improvement." They come to Zen because they want to accomplish more or become "better" people.

Finally, of course, there are people who practice Zen for spiritual reasons. These people want to experience *satori* or *kensho*. "Satori" literally means awakening, and "kensho" literally means seeing into our true nature. This seeing is done not with our eyes but with our whole body and mind.

All these reasons are valid. Zen can help you restore balance to your life. Zen can be beneficial for your health. Zen can help you sift through your own priorities, so you can get more done.

Zen can also improve your psychological health. The practice of Zen doesn't eliminate conflict and strife, but it does help put our problems in perspective. Zen practice gives stability, so that when we get knocked over, when something unexpected sends us reeling, we bounce back and recover our balance faster.

The practice of Zen can help us in many other ways as well. It can give us an experience of inner peace; it can strengthen our concentration. It can help us learn how to let go of our preconceptions and biases. It can teach us ways to work more efficiently. These are all beneficial effects—but in a sense, they are still all "side effects."

At its deepest, most basic level, Zen—or any spiritual path, for that matter—is much more than a list of what we can get from it. In fact, Zen is the realization of the oneness of life in all its aspects. It's not just the pure or "spiritual" part of life: it's the whole thing. It's flowers, mountains, rivers, streams, *and* the inner city and homeless children on Forty-second Street. It's the empty sky and the cloudy sky and the smoggy sky, too. It's the pigeon flying in the empty sky, the pigeon shitting in the empty sky, and walking through the pigeon droppings on the sidewalk. It's the rose growing in the garden, the cut rose shining in the vase in the living room, the garbage where we throw away the rose, and the compost where we throw away the garbage.

Zen is life—our life. It's coming to the realization that all things are nothing but expressions of myself. And myself is nothing but the full expression of all things. It's a life without limits.

There are many different metaphors for such a life. But the one that I have found the most useful, and the most meaningful, comes from the kitchen. Zen masters call a life that is lived fully and completely, with nothing held back, "the supreme meal." And a person who lives such a life—a person who knows how to plan, cook, appreciate, serve, and offer the supreme meal of life, is called a Zen cook.

The position of the cook is one of the highest and most important in the Zen monastery. During the thirteenth century, Dogen, the founder of the largest Zen Buddhist school in Japan, wrote a famous manual called "Instructions to the Cook." In this book, he recounted how he had taken the perilous sea voyage to China to find a true master. When he finally reached his destination, having survived typhoons and pirates, he was forced to wait aboard his ship while the Chinese officials examined his papers.

One day, an elderly Chinese monk came to the ship. He was the *tenzo*, or head cook, of his monastery, he told Dogen, and because the next day was a holiday, the first day of spring, he wanted to offer the monks something special. He had walked twelve miles to see if he could buy some of the renowned shiitake mushrooms Dogen had brought from Japan to add to the noodle soup he was planning to serve the next morning.

Dogen was very impressed with this monk, and he asked him to stay for dinner and spend the night.

But the monk insisted he had to return to the monastery immediately.

"But surely," said Dogen, "there are other monks who could prepare the meal in your absence."

"I have been put in charge of this work," replied the monk. "How can I leave it to others?"

"But why does a venerable elder such as yourself waste time doing the hard work of a head cook?" Dogen persisted. "Why don't you spend your time practicing meditation or studying the words of the masters?"

The Zen cook burst out laughing, as if Dogen had said something very funny. "My dear foreign friend," he said, "it's clear you do not yet understand what Zen practice is all about. When you get the chance, please come and visit me at my monastery so we can discuss these matters more fully."

And with that, he gathered up his mushrooms and began the long journey back to his monastery.

Dogen did eventually visit and study with the Zen cook in his monastery, as well as with many other masters. When he finally returned to Japan, Dogen became a celebrated Zen master. But he never forgot the lessons he learned from the Zen cook in China. It was the Zen cook's duty, Dogen wrote, to make the best and most sumptuous meal possible out of whatever ingredients were available—even if he had only rice and water. The Zen cook used what he had rather than complaining or making excuses about what he didn't have.

On one level, Dogen's "Instructions to the Cook" is about the proper way to prepare and serve meals for the monks. But on another level it is about the supreme meal—our own life—which is both the greatest gift we can receive and the greatest offering we can make.

I practiced Zen and studied Dogen's instructions for many years to learn how to become a Zen cook who can prepare this supreme meal. I got up early, around five-thirty every morning, and sat in *zazen,* or Zen meditation, for many hours. With my teacher I studied *koans*—paradoxical Zen sayings such as "What is the sound of one hand clapping." Eventually I received transmission to teach in the Zen school Dogen had founded.

The principles I learned from my study of Zen—the principles of the Zen cook—can be used by anyone as a guide to living a full life, in the marketplace, in the home, and in the community.

A master chef spends many years serving an apprenticeship, preparing and serving thousands of meals. Some chefs keep their recipes and methods secret. But other chefs are willing to distill their years of experience—including failures, mistakes, and successes—into recipes that everyone can use to cook their own meals. In this book I have distilled my years of experience as a Zen cook and included in it my principles and recipes for the supreme meal of life.

Zen is based on the teachings of the Buddha. The Buddha was not God, or another name for God, or even a god. The Buddha was a human being who had an experience of awakening through his own effort. The Buddha's awakening or enlightenment came about through the practice of meditation.

What did the Buddha discover? There are many different answers to this question. But the Zen tradition I studied says simply that when the Buddha attained realization, he opened his eyes to see the morning star shining in the sky and exclaimed, "How wonderful, how wonderful! Everything is enlightened. All beings and all things are enlightened just as they are."

So the first principle of the Zen cook is that we already have everything we need. If we look closely at our lives, we will find that we have all the ingredients we need to prepare the supreme meal. At every moment, we simply take the ingredients at hand and make the best meal we can. It doesn't matter how much or how little we have. The Zen cook just looks at what is available and starts with that.

The supreme meal of my life has taken many surprising forms. I have been an aeronautical engineer and a Zen student and teacher. I have also been an entrepreneur who founded a successful bakery and a social activist who founded the Greyston Family Inn, providing permanent housing and training in self-sufficiency for homeless families. I'm also involved in starting an AIDS hospice and an interfaith center.

Of course, the supreme meal is very different for each of us. But according to the principles of the Zen cook, it always consists of five main "courses" or aspects of life. The first course involves spirituality; the second course is composed of study and learning; the third course deals with livelihood; the fourth course is made out of social action or change, and the last course consists of relationship and community.

All these courses are an essential part of the supreme meal. Just as we all need certain kinds of food to make a complete meal that will sustain and nourish us, we need all five of these courses to live a full life.

It's not enough to simply include all these courses in our meal. We have to prepare the five courses at the right time and in the right order.

The first course, spirituality, helps us to realize the oneness of life and provides a still point at the center of all our activities. This course consists of certain spiritual practices. This practice could be prayer or listening to music or dance or taking walks or spending time alone—anything that helps us realize or reminds us of the oneness of life—of what Buddha meant when he said, "How wonderful, how wonderful."

The second course is study or learning. Study provides sharpness and intelligence. People usually study before they begin something, but I like my study of things, be they livelihood, social action, or spirituality, to be simultaneous with my practice of livelihood, social action, or spirituality. In this way, study is never merely abstract.

Once we have established the clarity that comes from stillness and study, we can begin to see how to prepare the third course, which is livelihood. This is the course that sustains us in the physical world. It is the course of work and business—the meat and potatoes. Taking care of ourselves and making a living in the world are necessary and important for all of us, no matter how "spiritual" we may think we are.

The course of social action grows naturally out of the courses of spirituality and livelihood. Once we begin to take care of our own basic needs, we become more aware of the needs of the people around us. Recognizing the oneness of life, we naturally reach out to other people because we realize that we are not separate from them.

The last course is the course of relationship and community. This is the course that brings all the seemingly separate parts of our life together into a harmonious whole. It's the course that turns all the other courses—spirituality, livelihood, social action, and study—into a joyous feast.

All the courses make up the supreme meal of our life. But it is not a question of trying to arrange our life so that we prepare equal amounts of each course. We all need different ingredients, and different amounts, at different times in our lives.

At this point in your life, maybe you need to focus on your livelihood, or perhaps you need to focus on spirituality. You have to reevaluate your situation constantly. You don't make a satisfying meal by using equal amounts of salt and sugar. You need to look at your situation and find out how much of each ingredient is needed at any given moment.

PAINTED CAKES ARE REAL, TOO

The supreme meal is a metaphor. We usually say that metaphors are not the same as the reality they describe. We say, for example, that "the map is not the territory." Or—as the Zen saying goes—"you can't eat painted cakes."

This is true, as far as it goes. But like most truths, it is really only a half or perhaps three-quarter truth. Dogen went deeper when he wrote in his greatest work, the *Shobogenzo*, that "painted cakes are real, too." Maps, recipes, and instruction manuals are made up of real words and images that convey real information about our lives and the world we live in. A map can help us get from here to there; a recipe can help us bake a delicious loaf of bread; and words that come from experience and the heart can help us to live more fully and completely.

So this book is my painted cake. My hope is that it will help you to discover and practice the ancient and yet up-to-date principles of the Zen cook so that you can prepare the supreme meal for yourself and others, moment after moment. For the supreme meal—your own life—is the greatest gift you can receive and the greatest offering you can make.

RECIPES FOR SPIRIT

1
THE MAKING OF A ZEN COOK

I first came across Zen Buddhism in a college course on religion. We were reading Huston Smith's textbook, *The Religions of Man.* There was only one page on Zen Buddhism. But that page felt like home to me. At that time, there were no Zen teachers or Zen centers in New York—or anywhere else in the country as far as I knew. But I read everything I could find on the subject, which in those days meant I read books by Alan Watts and D. T. Suzuki.

I graduated from the Polytechnic Institute of Brooklyn in 1960 with a degree in aeronautical engineering. Just after graduation, I was sitting with a classmate in a pizza parlor, talking about what we were going to do with our lives. I said, without thinking too much about it, that I had three goals:

First, I said, I wanted to study Zen in a monastery.

Second, I wanted to experience communal living on a kibbutz.

And third, I wanted to live as a bum on the Bowery.

Thirty years later, I have accomplished all three of these goals, though in ways I couldn't have imagined at the time. A year or so after graduation, I did spend a year at a kibbutz in Israel. And I did study Zen in a monastery, although it wasn't in Japan, which is probably how I imagined it in that pizza parlor. It was in the heart of downtown Los Angeles, and it was more of a Zen center than a monastery, though we practiced meditation as hard as most monks in most monasteries. And now I've achieved my last goal of living as a bum on the Bowery, though it was only for a week. I did it as part of my training for working with the homeless.

I didn't know it at the time, of course, but those three goals—these three wishes—made so casually during a college bull session in a pizza parlor more than thirty years ago were actually the seeds that would eventually grow into my supreme meal.

Living on a kibbutz in Israel gave me a deep appreciation and interest in the power of community—and family. On the boat to Israel I met my first wife, Helen, the daughter of an orthodox rabbi and businessman. I returned to America to take a job with McDonnell-Douglas in Los Angeles, and I worked as a project manager on the manned mission to Mars.

My work was exciting and fulfilling. But somehow my curiosity about Zen continued to grow. Since I couldn't just take off for Japan—I had a good job and a family to support, after all—I read books and stayed up late into the night, smoking cigars and talking about Zen and similar subjects with like-minded friends. Then I discovered a small Zen temple right in my own backyard, in Little Tokyo. The name of the temple was Zenshu-ji, and it was a branch temple of the Soto school of Zen. I was later to learn that this was the school that Dogen had founded after encountering the Zen cook in China.

Looking back now, I can also see that I was already following the first principle of the Zen cook—I was beginning with the ingredients that were right in front of me.

The Zen instruction at Zenshu-ji in those days was very low-key. The head of the temple held a small *zazenkai*—a Zen meditation sitting—once a week, on Sunday mornings. In contrast to the late-night talks and arguments about Zen I was having with my friends, there wasn't much talk here. We didn't "discuss" Zen or analyze it or theorize about it either, for that matter. We just did it. Most of the instruction was about the physical posture of how to sit. We sat on little round black cushions, called *zafus,* facing the wall. We crossed our legs as best we could and kept our backs straight, our hands folded in our laps, thumbs just touching, and our eyes half opened. We were instructed to focus on our breathing by silently counting from one to ten over and over again. If we lost count, or if we went past ten (I once got to a hundred before I became aware of it), we were instructed to return to one and start over again. It was very simple but also very demanding. In between sittings, we did walking meditation.

There was a young Zen monk visiting from Japan, who spoke a little English. His name was Taizan Maezumi, and he would eventually become my roshi, or Zen teacher. One day, after sitting, I asked him what I should be doing during walking meditation. He looked at me and said, "When we walk, we just walk."

A few months later, I attended a weekend meditation retreat with Yasutani Roshi, a visiting Zen master from Japan. Yasutani Roshi gave each of us a *koan* to meditate on. Three times a day, we went into a little room to give him our response. The young monk was translating for him. After the retreat, I asked the young monk if I could study with him. He said that he hadn't yet finished his studies, but that I should just continue sitting.

Eventually, the young monk started a Zen center in a little house in downtown Los Angeles, and I began to sit with him. In those days, I would get up early to practice meditation and then carpool to work at McDonnell-Douglas. Then I'd return to my house near the Zen center and attend the evening sitting. Whenever I could, I would take time off to practice meditation for longer periods.

HUNGRY GHOSTS

Meditation was the heart of our practice. But we also practiced chanting and bowing. During meditation retreats, we ate our meals in the *zendo*—the meditation hall—so that even eating became part of our meditation. Before eating, we offered some food to the Buddha, the teaching, and the community. And after each meal, we offered leftovers to the hungry ghosts.

In Buddhism, the hungry ghosts are pictured as miserable creatures who have huge, swollen bellies and needle-thin necks. Even though they are surrounded by food, they can never satisfy their hunger or thirst because they can eat or drink only one drop of food at a time. Their necks are thin as needles because they are so caught up in their conditioning that they can't accept or appreciate the food that is actually in front of them.

Actually, we are all hungry ghosts. It's a metaphor for the part of us that's unsatisfied. Because of our attachments and our conditioning, we miss the food and drink that's right in front of us. In fact, the ingredients we need to make a meal that will satisfy us are all right here. But we refuse to accept the food that's offered. We get taken over by the feeling that we can't do what needs to be done. So we're always looking for something we don't have. Somehow we can't just say, "Let's take all this and make a wonderful feast." It all comes down to a very human habit: we're always looking for something beyond what is right in front of us.

Hungry ghosts manifest themselves in all sorts of ways. I myself experienced the immense hunger that we all have one morning while I was riding in my car pool to work. I had been practicing meditation intensively during the early mornings when I suddenly realized the universality of hunger. I felt this great hunger all around me. I saw that even though there is enough food in our society to feed everyone, many, many people hunger for food. I saw that even though some people have more than enough food, they hunger for power. I saw that some of us thirst for appreciation or fame. Others are starved for love. And spiritual seekers, including Zen students, crave enlightenment.

As soon as I felt this great thirsting, I made a vow. I vowed to dedicate my life to offering the supreme meal to all of us hungry ghosts in the ten directions.

This is the vow of the Zen cook. In Zen, a vow is not something we promise to do and then feel bad or guilty about if we don't accomplish it. Rather, a vow is an *intention* to do something.

Many of us think we have to limit our meal because the ingredients we have on hand—whether food, money, time, talent, intelligence, or energy—are limited.

But a vow is not limited, either by space or time. We can make our vows as small or as large as we want. We can make a vow to feed one person, for instance, or we can make a vow to feed hundreds or thousands of people. We can vow to build housing for one homeless person or for hundreds or thousands of families. We can even vow to end hunger or homelessness. The only thing that limits our vow is our imagination.

But even though a vow has no limits, a vow has a very practical function: it's like a compass that shows us the direction to go in and that keeps us on course. But a vow by itself is never enough. By itself, a vow is all potential. It's like yeast or starter. But if we want to see our vow manifest in the world, if we want to bake a real loaf of bread, one that we can eat ourselves and serve to others, we have to add flour and water and knead them all together. We have to add determination.

When we add determination, vision takes on a life and force of its own. The loaf of bread we imagined comes out of the oven, ready to eat.

COOKING COOKS

As the Zen center grew, I threw myself into my Zen practice with more and more intensity. I worked on hundreds of different koans, both with my teacher and with his teachers, who occasionally came from Japan to lead meditation retreats. As my own practice progressed, I was given more and more responsibility. Finally I left my job and became a full-time monk. In 1976, I became my teacher's first heir. Everything was done in a traditional way. I even went to Japan, where I served as abbot of the two main monasteries of the Soto school for one night.

This meant that I was officially registered as a Zen teacher in Japan.

When I returned from Japan, I began to lead retreats myself under the watchful eye of my teacher. But I also helped start a number of other programs. We opened a neighborhood clinic that served a diverse urban neighborhood. We started a publishing company, specializing in books about Zen practice. We also ran a landscaping and carpentry business and bought and rehabilitated an apartment building on an adjacent block.

All this activity might surprise people who think that Zen or spirituality represents a passive retreat from life. But activity is actually a very important part of Zen. The insight and equanimity that can come from spiritual practice should open our eyes to the problems of people around us and make us more effective.

In 1979, I returned to New York to start a Zen community with my wife and family and a few students. We had almost no resources, but from the very beginning our vision was very big—immense, in fact.

I knew from the beginning that we would have to form a community that included and integrated all the "main courses" of life. We began with the course of spirituality. The practice of Zen was our spiritual touchstone.

Next came the second course, the course of livelihood. We wanted to develop a way to make a living, a livelihood, that would help others as well as ourselves. And we wanted to become involved in our community—in the world of social action—in a way that would transform the lives of the people we were helping.

So I didn't want to start a business that would

provide work for just a few Zen students and help support just our community. I wanted to start a business that could also provide jobs and job training outside our community. But more than that, I was looking for a way for business itself to become a force for social change and a way of spiritual transformation.

Our vision for the third course, social action, was also very large. We didn't want to feed just a few people. We wanted to end homelessness altogether—first in Yonkers, where we lived and worked, and then in the rest of the country. A few years after moving to New York, the Zen community formed the Greyston Family Inn and bought an abandoned apartment building at 68 Warburton Avenue. Two years later, the Greyston Builders—a minority construction company founded to handle renovations—finished work on 68 Warburton, and eighteen families moved into their new apartments and began a process of education, counseling, and job training. And now we have begun renovating two more apartment buildings.

In all these projects, I was looking for a way to accomplish my vow to offer the supreme meal to all sentient beings.

From one point of view, of course, such a vow is impossible to accomplish. There are simply too many hungry ghosts in this world with too many needs. No one can cook such a meal alone. But the Zen cook doesn't try to cook this meal by himself or herself. The Zen cook is always cooking other cooks who teach other cooks, and so on—infinitely. In this way, one person can have a tremendous effect. A simple meal can become transformed into a great feast.

2

HOW TO COOK

When Dogen asked the Zen cook from the Chinese temple why he didn't have his assistants do the hard work of drying mushrooms in the hot sun, the cook said, "I am not other people." In the same way, we have to realize that this life is the only life we have. It's ours, right now. If we don't do the cooking ourselves, we are throwing our life away. "Keep your eyes open," Dogen instructs. "Wash the rice thoroughly, put it in the pot, light the fire, and cook it. There is an old saying that goes, 'See the pot as your own head, see the water as your lifeblood.'"

When we cook—and live—with this kind of attention, the most ordinary acts and the humblest ingredients are revealed as they truly are. "Handle even a single leaf of a green in such a way that it manifests the body of the Buddha," says Dogen. "This in turn allows the Buddha to manifest through the leaf."

TRANSFORMATION

Cooking, like life, is about transformation. When we cook, we work directly with the elemental forces of fire and heat, water, metal, and clay. We put the lid on the pot and wait for the fire to transform the rice, or we mix the bread with yeast and put it in the oven to bake. There is something hidden, almost magical about it.

This kind of transformation involves a certain amount of faith. We work hard to prepare the food. We wash the rice, knead the bread, and break the eggs. We measure the ingredients carefully. We mix, stir, blend. But then we have to wait. We have to let fire and water transform the food we've prepared.

But we also have to keep an eye on things. We have to be aware of what is going on. For the Zen cook the old adage "A watched pot never boils" is only half true. We leave the lid on the pot most of the time. But we also lift the lid every once in a while to taste the food.

The Zen cook follows the middle way. We have faith that the soup is coming along—but we still check now and then.

The accomplished Zen cook is something of an alchemist. He or she can transform poisons into virtues.

The Zen cook doesn't do this by adding a secret ingredient but by leaving something out. The Zen cook leaves out our attachment to the self.

For example, anger is considered a poison when it is self-motivated and self-centered. But take that attachment to the self out of anger, and the same emotion becomes the fierce energy of determination, which is a very positive force. Take the self-centered aspect out of greed, and it becomes the desire to help. Drop the self-orientation from ignorance, and it becomes a state of unknowing that allows new things to arise.

INGREDIENTS

How do we find the ingredients? We simply open our eyes and look around us. We take the materials that are at hand, right in front of us, and prepare the best meal possible. We work with what we have in each and every moment.

Our body is an ingredient. Our relationships are ingredients. Our thoughts, our emotions, and all our actions are ingredients.

The place we live, the leaves that fall, the haze around the moon, the traffic in the city streets, the corner market—all these are also our ingredients. In order to see the ingredients in front of us, we have to open our eyes. Usually we create our own boundaries, our own small view, our own territory, and that's the only place we look. With practice, our territory expands, and all the objects of the world become our ingredients.

As we see ourselves as the world, as we see the oneness of life, the whole world becomes available. Then the Zen cook knows that every aspect of life is an ingredient of the supreme meal.

USE EVERYTHING

Our natural tendency is not to use ingredients we think might ruin our meal. We want to throw them away or maybe move them way back on the shelf, out of sight, behind everything else. But Dogen instructs us to take the ingredients we think are going to ruin our meal and figure out how to use them so that they improve it.

If something doesn't seem to work as a main course, for example, it might become an appetizer or a dessert. You can't just say, "I don't want it to be like that. I'll leave it out." That's a kind of denial. It's going to be there, whether you like it or not.

Take a group of people starting a new company. Their first step might be to take an inventory of their gifts. But if you decide you don't want the gifts one person has, you could be creating a problem, because his or her gifts are part of the company. In any case, that person's gifts will wind up getting used because they are part of the person. The question is how to use them. If you don't find a way, the person will end up jealous or resentful or bored. The unused gifts will wind up working to rot the company from the inside.

Let's say, for example, that someone is aggressive. But that energy might be just what's needed for certain difficult jobs—dealing with recalcitrant bureaucrats, for example. Or perhaps someone is so preoccupied with details that they are unable to see the larger picture. You wouldn't put that person on your five-year-planning committee. But they might be perfect as an accountant keeping track of daily receipts.

Sometimes it might seem that we can't find a way to use someone's particular qualities, which may seem toxic or harmful to our goal. In that case, we make a clear decision not to use their particular ingredient in the meal we are cooking. But we don't ignore or deny the ingredient. We acknowledge it, we're aware of it, we may even appreciate it in another context. But we just decide to use zero amount of it at the moment.

NONREJECTION

No matter who we are, we tend to reject someone or something.

When we first moved to the East Coast, before we began our bakery in Yonkers, we ran the food concession at the exclusive Riverdale Yacht Club. Some Zen students thought cooking gourmet meals and learning to set the table properly didn't really constitute traditional *samu*, or work practice, as did weeding the monastery garden or chopping wood. Many of our members said, "How can you serve the rich? What kind of a thing is that for a Zen center to do?"

Rejection can take many forms. We should not exclude the rich just because we think it is somehow nobler or more spiritual to work with the poor. The Zen student who rejects the rich person has the same problem as the rich person who rejects the Zen student. If you can work with what you reject, it turns out that you're working with yourself, with those parts of yourself that you've rejected. If I can learn to work with a rich person whom I've rejected, for example, then I can begin dealing with the richness rather than the poverty in myself.

The same principle holds true for business-people who reject their competitors or social activists who reject working with the government. In every area, working with what you habitually reject is one of the best ways to facilitate growth and transformation. Try to connect with the person you are rejecting or who seems to be rejecting you. When you try to see the world through your opponent's eyes, you have taken the first step toward turning enemies into friends or even allies.

When we first started Greyston Inn, Jack Meehan, who was in charge of a large private foundation, said to me, "Don't get involved with government. Get all your money from private sources. Then you can do whatever you want." But to me, the government was one of the ingredients. Even if they were an obstacle, I needed to learn how to cook with them.

Some people said, "Don't get involved with the politicians. They'll mess everything up." But to me, the politicians were also one of the ingredients, and I had to learn how to cook with them, too, as tough and difficult to work with as they might be.

I don't try to change the ingredients, though. I'm not trying to change conservatives into liberals or liberals into conservatives. Dogen says that every meal has to include a harmony of the six tastes—bitter, sour, sweet, hot, salty, and plain. None of these is better or more important than the others. Each ingredient has a different taste and a different reason for being part of the meal. They're all important.

TOO MUCH ZEN

Most of the time, we worry about not having enough of any given ingredient. But the Zen cook is also aware of the danger of having too much. In fact, having too much can be one of the greatest traps of all. Too much of a good thing can ruin a meal very quickly.

The cook who is too taken with the ingredient of spirituality could be afraid to get his or her hands dirty. He or she will never break an egg or cut a vegetable. If the cook is too involved with this ingredient, our ordinary everyday existence could be seen as an illusion, as if nothing matters. The cook begins to sound like Alfred E. Newman, the *Mad Magazine* cover boy: "What, me worry?" The cook is so aloof, so above it all, that either nothing happens and the meal never gets cooked or the meal is so thin and airy that it has no substance or body.

People who cling to the experience of spirituality are said to have "the stink of enlightenment." It's necessary to come back and work in the world.

SPICE

Cooks have different tastes. Some like bland food, others lots of spices. I'm one of those people who like spicy food. I don't feel comfortable unless I'm taking a risk.

The kind of risk I like to take is the risk that comes with making the fundamental changes that lead to a more enlightened society. It's the risk that comes with being what entrepreneur Bob Schwartz calls an "agent of change." When I see a need, I'm driven to do something about it—without being overly concerned about whether or not I have enough resources in hand.

Cooks who have a taste for the spice of risk can't be afraid of failure. People think they've failed when something doesn't work out the way they expected it to work out. But most things don't work out the way we expect them to.

That's not to say that we shouldn't try to make things happen the way we want them to, or even the way we hope they will. But we can't *expect* that they'll happen that way. We constantly have to take another look at the situation. Maybe something didn't happen because it wasn't the right time. Maybe something didn't happen because the right people hadn't come together, or maybe the circumstances weren't right. Maybe it will take another ten or fifty or a hundred years. The world always unfolds in its own way.

3

CLEANING KITCHEN IS CLEANING MIND

Right now, right in front of us, we have everything we need to begin.

Usually, when we want to begin a new project—whether it be a new business or a new relationship or a new life—we're in a hurry. We want to jump right in and do something—anything. But the Zen cook knows that we can't prepare a meal if the kitchen is cluttered with last night's dishes. In order to see the ingredients we already have in our lives, we need to clear a space. "Clean the chopsticks, ladles, and all other utensils," Dogen advises. "Handle them with equal care and awareness, putting everything back where it naturally belongs."

So we always begin by cleaning. Even if the kitchen looks clean, we still have to clean it again each time we want to start a new meal. It's like taking a glass from the cupboard. We wipe it off before giving it to a guest.

The cleaning process itself changes the cook as well as the surroundings and the people who come into those surroundings—whether we're in a Zen meditation hall, a living room, a kitchen, or an office. That is why so much emphasis is placed on cleaning in a Zen monastery. It doesn't matter whether we think anything is dirty or not. We just clean.

The process of cleaning also allows us to discover the ingredients that are already in this space. We begin to see the ingredients we already have. Before we start to reclean the shelves, for instance, we have to take out the jars. In doing so, we see all the jars we have and find that some are empty, some are almost empty, and others are full. We find out what we don't need, what we have too much of, what's been spoiled, and what needs to be thrown away.

Of course cleaning is an ideal that is never satisfied. Therefore, because we can't fully clean, what we have left becomes part of the ingredients of each new meal. Because we can't clean that glass, our new actions are preconditioned by that dirty glass. So we practice to make each new action as clean and unconditioned as possible.

CLEANING THE MIND

Our lives work the same way. Just as we start cooking a meal by cleaning the kitchen, it's helpful to start the day by cleaning our mind. In Zen Buddhism, we clean the mind by the process of meditation, or *zazen*, which literally means "just sitting."

For me, *zazen* is an activity like sleeping, eating, drinking, and going to the bathroom: if I don't take care of these natural functions, I feel a difference in myself. If I don't eat, for example, I start getting very hungry, and if I don't sleep, I feel tired. And if I don't sit, my stability decreases, and I feel uncentered.

We don't practice to attain enlightenment, just as we don't eat or breathe to be alive. Because we're alive, we breathe. Because we're alive, we eat. Because we're enlightened, we do *zazen*. Dogen says that *zazen* is a manifestation of the enlightened state. We practice and recognize everything we do as a manifestation of the enlightened state.

The basic ingredients are very simple:

A space to meditate in.

A cushion or chair to meditate on.

And your body and mind.

Choose a time of day when your chances of being interrupted are minimal—early morning, before most people have gotten up, for example.

Find a space that is quiet, not too dark or too light, and where you are not likely to be disturbed. If necessary, close the door.

Make the space aesthetically pleasing. Depending on your taste, include an inspiring image, or a natural object such as a beautiful rock or flower. Candles and incense are optional as well.

Wear comfortable, nonbinding clothes.

Assume a comfortable position. Back erect and without tension. Do not lean against the wall or the back of the chair.

Place your right hand, palm up, on your lap and left hand, palm up, on your right hand, thumbs slightly touching. This position is called the cosmic mudra and creates a restful environment for the mind.

If you are sitting on a chair, place your feet squarely on the ground with knees approximately six inches apart.

If you are sitting on a cushion (a folded blanket will also do nicely), adjust the height of the cushion so that both knees rest firmly on the ground. The equilateral triangle formed by this position gives support to both the back and spinal column.

Let your eyes remain half closed, half open, lightly resting on a spot on the floor approximately three feet in front of you. This will allow your eye muscles to relax while you keep an alert state of mind.

Place the tip of your tongue at the top of your palate, behind your top front teeth. Keep your mouth closed and breathe through the nose.

Concentrate on your breathing. Notice inhalation and exhalation. As you inhale, count one. As you exhale, count two. Continue to ten, and then repeat from one to ten again.

As thoughts arise, let them come and go. Keep your attention on the counting. When you notice that thoughts have distracted you and you have lost your count, gently return to the counting. Start over at one.

Continue for a minimum of two and a maximum of thirty minutes.

Repeat daily—or at least once a week.

CLEARING THE LAKE

When talking about *zazen,* I like to use the metaphor of the moon on the lake. Our thoughts and emotions are like the ripples and waves that disturb the reflective surface of the lake, so that we can't see the moon. Of course the moon is always there, even if we can't see it, and it's also important to see the ripples. But we still need to see the moon clearly to know it's there. So in meditation, when we let the ripples of our thoughts and the waves of our emotions settle, it's as if we have cleared the lake so that the moon can appear.

A PLACE FOR EVERYBODY

When we first moved to New York to establish our community, the first thing we did was make a *zendo.* We tried to design a meditation room that wouldn't exclude anybody, since I didn't want to limit our community to Buddhists. We used an empty room, with no Buddhas or any other images. It was simply a place for sitting in silence. We hoped it would be a place where anyone—Buddhists, Christians, Jews, Moslems, Hindus, or atheists—would feel welcome to meditate or pray or just experience the silence in their own way.

Of course, it wasn't that easy. We had to have something to sit on. We chose black cushions, which is what Zen Buddhists usually sit on. But some people felt that it was too somber and serious. Then some of the Buddhists didn't like the fact that we had no image of the Buddha, and so on.

In fact, it was a good learning experience. It reminded us of one of the basic principles of the Zen cook—that it's in the nature of form to exclude other forms. As soon as you create something, you create a boundary. No matter how deep our sense of egolessness is, or how far we can extend our sense of interconnectedness, we still feel some kind of separation. And the practice, the path, in trying to eliminate that boundary, then creates a new one. The trick, I think, is to be aware of this so that you can either expand the boundary or perhaps create another way to take care of the aspect that has been left out.

START BY DOING NOTHING

Like most busy executives, I get up very early. But I don't use that time to read the papers, or make phone calls, or prepare for meetings later in the day. No matter how busy I get, I always try to start the day by sitting in meditation.

Although we had a meditation hall as a central

part of our community, when we established our bakery we also set aside a place for meditation. We built a *zendo*— a meditation hall—upstairs and we practiced meditation there every morning from five-thirty to seven, before starting work.

Of course, not everyone has the room for a separate meditation space. But that shouldn't stop us. At the office of Greyston Family Inn, the administrative center of our work with the homeless, we also start each day sitting around the conference table in silence for fifteen minutes or so before we begin our morning meetings. And at 68 Warburton, our tenant organization begins their meetings with a few minutes of silence.

The silence of meditation can have tremendous power. When I spoke at an interfaith group preparing resolutions for the UN, I suggested that we all ask the members of our groups to set aside one minute of silent meditation at noon for peace. Can you imagine the whole world stopping for one minute? My conviction is that if the whole world were to sit still for one minute, it would do more for the cause of world peace than ten years of negotiations.

One of the participants of that meeting, Brother David Steindl-Rast, a Benedictine monk, has observed that minute of silence at noon for ten years now. He reminds himself by setting his watch alarm. But "noon" can come at any time. When our bakery was on a night schedule, we observed our minute of silence at midnight.

The emptiness of meditation does not denote a lack or absence of anything but is actually the state of openness that makes all things possible. It is like the space inside a cup or the space at the hub of the wheel. A full cup can't receive anything, but an empty cup can receive all kinds of offerings. And a wheel without a hub for an axle cannot turn.

This "empty" space is completely awake and alive. All the forms and energies of the world arise from it, like clouds arising in a bright blue sky.

A PLACE FOR EVERYTHING

We often think that to be spiritual or enlightened we need to have some special experiences, just as we think that in order to make a great meal or become a master chef we need special ingredients and a fancy kitchen. But all we have to do to make a meal is put all the pots and pans and ingredients in their proper places. And all we have to do to be in touch with our spirituality is to let the mind settle itself, like a cloudy glass of city tap water.

The Japanese sometimes describe ordinariness as orderliness. Order creates simplicity based on how things naturally are or work. As Dogen says, "Put those things that naturally go on a high place onto a high place and those that would be most stable on a low place onto a low place; things that naturally belong on a high place settle on a high place, while those that belong on a low place find their greatest stability there." In the kitchen in the Zen monastery, for example, the knives hang next to the cutting block and the bucket hangs next to the well. When the monks take off their shoes before entering the meditation hall, they not only line them up neatly, they line them up facing away from the meditation hall, so that when they slip them on for walking meditation, they are pointing in the right direction.

It doesn't matter if we have only a few essential things or many things. It doesn't make a difference whether we are working in a very simple kitchen or a very fancy kitchen filled with automatic bread-making machines, a microwave oven, and all the latest conveniences. We still have to put everything in order, in its right place. When we do that, we'll have an orderly kitchen and an ordinary mind.

A monk once asked Zen master Baso, "What is Buddha-Mind?" The master replied, "Ordinary mind." Meditation allows things to fall in all the right places so that we can see clearly what comes up in the mind and let go of our judgments. We don't say, "I won't eat salt today, so I'm going to throw the salt out." We just put the salt where it belongs. In the same way, we have to let things settle in our lives. When we do that, we find that we have created a space in which everything can find its own space. Our ordinary mind, with everything naturally settled in its right place, is actually the enlightened mind.

PUT PEOPLE IN THE RIGHT PLACE

In the Greyston Bakery we apply this principle in developing our job-training program. When we hire new workers, we take all their capabilities into account. We try to put them in the proper place.

Many companies who would like to work with chronically unemployed and undertrained workers from the inner city make the mistake of beginning with the workplace and not the labor force. They build complicated automated production facilities and then complain that their workers can't run those facilities.

But we begin with the capabilities of the worker. We don't take someone with minimum knowledge and skills and place them in a position that requires high levels of skill. We create the production process to fit the capabilities of our workforce.

We didn't start out with a lot of expensive equipment. As our workers gained knowledge and expertise in simpler manual operations and as they learned better work habits, we upgraded our equipment. And our workers upgraded their skills.

THE CLUTTER OF CONDITIONING

What prevents us from seeing things and ourselves clearly is the clutter of our conditioning.

Conditioning, of course, is very natural, just as the ripples and waves on the lake are natural. Conditioning is due to previous events. When things happen a certain way a number of times, we form the habit of expecting things to continue happening that way. And so we act as we have in the past. But in actuality everything is always changing. No two moments are the same.

Meditation—or whatever technique of cleaning the mind we practice—can help free us from our conditioning by allowing us to let go of our attachments to the past.

It's important to realize, however, that we don't have to forget the past. We only have to let go of our attachments to the past. Let's say, for example, that I've done business with someone who has taken advantage of me five or six times. I shouldn't forget that. But at the same time, I don't have to be so attached to what happened in the past that it overwhelms what I think of that person now.

In Zen we have a saying that if you haven't

seen somebody for two minutes, don't assume he or she is the same person. Maybe that person has changed, or maybe conditions have changed. The important thing is to see what I can do now. If you and I are not bound by our past conditioning, we can see things afresh. Then every moment contains a new opportunity.

When we began working with the homeless, a community activist strongly opposed us. He called us "poverty pimps." He felt that we were bringing Afro-American women out of the motels for slave labor in the bakery, and that once we had gotten what we could get out of them, we would throw them back into the motels. When we tried to get a zoning clearance for the building to house the homeless, he came to the zoning board hearing and complained that we were running a scam to use government funds to enrich ourselves.

Over time, we began to get to know each other a little better, but he still was very negative about our work. Then one day he called wanting my support for a low-income housing project he was working on. My first instinct was to wonder what his real motives were.

But the situation had changed. He had seen the fruits of the work we had done. In fact, a relative of his had begun to work in our bakery. He wasn't calling to fight or complain. He was simply calling to ask our view about the project he was working on.

NOTHING IS MISSING

When we meditate, we begin to see the self-sufficiency of our own mind. We don't need to add all sorts of things. We don't need to build ourselves up. We don't even need to "improve" ourselves because we have everything we need right now. But we forget this. There is an old Buddhist story about a prince who was very handsome. Every morning, when he woke up, he would look at himself in the mirror and exclaim, "Ah! How beautiful!"

One day he woke up and picked up the mirror the wrong way. Because he was looking at the unpolished back of the mirror, he couldn't see his face. He ran out of his palace into the streets yelling, "My head is gone! My head is gone!" He went completely crazy, looking everywhere for his missing head.

Finally one of his friends found him and grabbed him. "Why are you running around like this?" his friend said. "Your head isn't missing."

"No, no, my head is gone. It's gone," the prince cried.

They took him back to the palace, but no matter what they said, they couldn't calm him down. Because they didn't have straitjackets in those days, they tied him to a pillar. Because he was screaming so much, they put a gag on him.

He kept struggling, but you can only struggle so long, and when he finally calmed down a little, his friend hit him in the face.

"My head is there, after all!" the prince shouted. He was beside himself with joy. For the next few days, he went around telling everybody how wonderful and miraculous it was that he had found his head. His friends just looked at him in disbelief. But it took a long time for him to stop being so exuberant about the fact that he had found the head that had been there all along.

Like the prince who thought he had lost his head, we sometimes run all over the place looking for what we already have. Zen is a practice that ties you up and makes you sit down and stay still.

That in itself is not enough, however. Once we've been tied down, we need to be jolted or startled. This jolt could be subtle, like the sound of a stone hitting a bamboo, or the sight of a falling peach blossom, or the morning star. Or it could be shocking, like the blow of a Zen master's stick, or stubbing your toe. Only then do we realize that we already have our head—that we have *always* had our head—and that, as Dogen says, "Everything as it is is the enlightened way."

ZEN WON'T SOLVE YOUR PROBLEMS

Zen can help you find your head, but it won't necessarily solve all your problems. I remember hearing a Zen master say, "Zen will never get rid of your problems. The best it can do is to teach you how to deal with them."

My mother-in-law happened to be in the room at that time, and she said, "Why get involved, then? What good is it if you're not going to get rid of your problems?"

The Zen cook doesn't believe in utopias. Problems will always arise, both in our individual life and in society. It's the Zen cook's job to cook a meal and then clean the dirty dishes. Some people might say that cleaning the dishes is solving the problem of dirty dishes. But it's not, because you are going to eat another meal. The work of the Zen cook is cooking meals and cleaning dishes. It's an endless process.

The basic problem, actually, is how to get rid of the idea that we're going to get rid of our problems.

Only then can we relate directly with the real issues of our life.

DON'T WAIT UNTIL YOU'RE ENLIGHTENED

The clarity of our vision determines the set of ingredients in front of us. Most of us—whether we think of ourselves as religious people or not—would agree that the more clearly we can see the situation we're in, the better our plans and actions will be. But that doesn't mean we can say, "Well, I'm not yet clear enough to see the ingredients, so I'm going to wait until I can see what they really are." Whatever we see, that's what we have to use. It doesn't matter what it is as long as it's what we see. Based on the clarity that we have right now, and based on whatever we can see, we can begin to act.

After I'd been studying with my teacher, Maezumi Roshi, for about three years, he asked me to give introductory talks at local colleges. I told him that I wasn't ready. I didn't know enough. But he wouldn't accept that. He said that you'll never get to that place where you think you have enough clarity to teach—but that's not a problem, because teaching is really learning.

At the same time, we have to keep on working to improve our clarity. I don't care if you are a Buddha. You can still improve your clarity.

DON'T CLEAN JUST TO CLEAN

We never get to the point of no longer needing to clean the glass. We wash the dishes, and then a new stack appears in a little while. The process is endless. It's never over.

But it's also very important to remember that we don't sweep the floor just to have a clean floor. We clean things so that we can use them. We sweep the floor so we can walk on it. We sponge the counter so that we can cut vegetables on it; we wash the pots and pans so we can cook in them; we wash the plates so we can serve the meal on them. And we clean our mind so that we can start each moment anew.

RECIPES FOR LEARNING

4
BEGINNER'S MIND

Most of us think we have to become experts before we can do anything. We read all kinds of books, go to seminars, seek out "expert" advice, and so on. And more often than not, we never get around to actually trying the skill we want to learn, let alone mastering it.

The Zen cook's approach to learning is very different. It is not the way of the expert but the way of the beginner. The proper attitude to have when we're learning something is called "Beginner's Mind."

One of the best exemplars of Beginner's Mind is a baby learning to walk. Babies don't read books about walking or go to walking seminars. They just stand up, take a step, and fall down. Then they do it all over again. They might get frustrated or angry when they fall, but they don't get discouraged. They don't say, "See, that proves that I can't walk! I'll never learn to walk. Walking is impossible!"

LEARN FROM FEAR

The more we see, the more there is to work with. We tend to feel that the further along the spiritual path we go, the closer we will come to some kind of pure, true self. But we don't want to accept that the other confused and seemingly impure part of us is *also* the true self. If we really accept the fact that "I'm deluded forever," then we either have to accept the fact that the "deluded" self has to be the true self or accept the fact that we'll *never* reach the true self.

This puts us in something of a quandary. If we're in Beginner's Mind, then we have to be open to the fact that this is it. But we don't want to accept that, so there's a lot of resistance. We have to be able to ride it out, like riding a wild bull. We have to go through the pain and learn from it.

Our tendency in life is to avoid things that frighten us. But in order to become whole, we need to go deeper and deeper into ourselves by reaching further and further into the things we fear.

TAKING OUR OWN INVENTORY

In our Zen community study program, we begin our study of the self by looking at our own characteristics and traits.

The notion of taking our own inventory is part of the twelve-step program developed by Alcoholics Anonymous. The fourth step asks participants to "take a fearless moral inventory of your character defects." The twelve-step program is very powerful and effective, and I've learned a lot from it, but I wasn't comfortable with the notion of "character defects." Our approach is a little different. We prefer to make an inventory of whatever *characteristics* we can pin down, without judging them as good or bad.

This is not so easy to do. Many of our ingredients are kept in the closet, like old clothes we're too embarrassed to wear or musty spices stored too long in the cupboard. Taking them out so that we can look at them openly, without judgments, takes a lot of courage. This is why the fourth step of the AA program uses the word "fearless."

However you see yourself is fine. Taking things out of the closet and sharing them with other people who are doing the same thing makes everything much more fluid and open.

Some people might see themselves as very limited. Others might see themselves as more than one, in an almost schizophrenic way. I, for example, could see myself as a Zen monk, a business executive, a social activist, or a husband and father. I could be Bernie, which is my given name, or Tetsugen, which is my monk's name, or Roshi, which is my Zen teacher's title. It's a very wide spectrum. Anything is possible.

After taking our characteristics out of the cupboard, we share them with the other people in our group. We talk openly about ourselves. And finally, we each create a picture or map of ourselves and present it to the group. This presentation can take any form. It could be a painting or a sculpture, a play or even a song.

Sharing the contents of our personal inventory in this very graphic way with another person helps us to see that our concept of our self is nothing more than our concept of our self. It helps bring things out, and once things are out in the open, we can either use them as ingredients or let go of our attachments to them so that they don't control us.

Sharing our inventory also helps us to see that we're not alone. We lose a lot of fear when we feel there's a group of people going through the same thing.

Meditation is a very important part of the inventory-taking process. It helps us to see the concepts we have of ourselves clearly and without judgment. At this point, that's all we're doing. We're not trying to get rid of our ideas about ourselves or the self. We're not worrying about getting in touch with our inner children, our true selves, or God, or any of the terms we have for enlightened states.

Like most of us, when I took my inventory in our study group, I found both "good" and "bad" characteristics. For example, I'm pushy. I'm very determined to get things done. If someone is hungry, I want to feed them. If someone is homeless, I want to find a place for them to live.

But this determination can come at the expense of relating to people with real sensitivity. When you're determined, you tend to move quickly. That can cause other people to stumble. In taking my inventory with other members of my community, I found that I don't thank or acknowledge people enough—because I always assume we should just keep going and do more.

I also tend to be stubborn. That's the negative side. The positive side is that I'm tenacious. I don't give up—I just wait until the right time, until events or circumstances move in the direction I want to go. Then I can move with the flow of things. It's like judo. Sometimes it can take a long time. When we first moved to Riverdale, for example, I knew that I wanted to be involved in interfaith work, but it wasn't the right time. Now, ten years later, circumstances have changed, and the time is right. We've begun work on an interfaith community, the House of One People (HOOP), involving Moslems, Catholics, Jews, Buddhists, and Hindus.

FROM CHARACTERISTICS TO INGREDIENTS

Once we see our characteristics clearly, we can recognize that they are our raw materials. They are our ingredients.

We work with our ingredients on a day-to-day basis by creating short-term goals that reflect the direction in which we want to go. Suppose I've decided that one of my characteristic ingredients is laziness—and that's keeping me from developing a spiritual discipline. I might make it a short-term goal to meditate for fifteen minutes a day, keeping a log to see how well I keep my discipline.

One morning I might get up out of bed as soon as my alarm goes off. Another morning I might stay in bed and just watch my reactions when the alarm clock goes off or when someone knocks on the door. At the end of three months, I might notice that sometimes I'm lazy and sometimes I'm not. We pay attention to that characteristic to see if it's really so, or how it changes. And once again, we share it with others. In this way, we become more familiar with our habits and how they function. We see them as ingredients rather than as problems to be solved.

LET GO AND ACCEPT

There are no intrinsically good or bad ingredients. Of course, there are ingredients I like and ingredients I don't like. There are ingredients that society likes and doesn't like. But all these likes and dislikes are very subjective. They are all a matter of personal taste.

It's human to make judgments, because we all have discriminating minds. And it's also human to hold on to those judgments. So when we find ourselves making judgments, we should bear in mind that whatever judgment we make is a subjective one we're making now, and that it could change.

We should realize making and holding judgments can create problems. Let's say it rains one day. If I had been planning a picnic, I might easily become angry at the rain for ruining my picnic. But the same rain might make me very happy the next day because it provided water for my garden.

So I can feel free to have feelings and make judgments about things, *and* I also can feel free not to hold on to those feelings and judgments. We are human, and circumstances will cause things to happen. Jealousy will arise, sadness will arise, happiness will arise.

Learning how to let go of these feelings becomes part of our meal. But to accept the arising of those same feelings is also part of our meal. We need to practice *both* letting go and accepting. When we do this we begin to taste what it's like to live in a state of freedom.

OUR FAULTS ARE OUR BEST INGREDIENTS

As soon as we look at our faults or weaknesses as ingredients, we gain a different perspective. The things we are used to thinking of as faults tend to be the very things we can use to make delicious meals. But they're tricky to use, like chili or hot pepper. We have to work with them carefully.

Our faults can be seen as great resources. This means knowing how they function, without further confusing ourselves by making judgments. This is a hard habit to break, but well worth the effort.

The characteristics we consider faults are all ours. If we are lazy, for example, we don't have to make a special effort or *try* to be lazy. If we are hot tempered, we don't need to develop our propensity for anger. We're already that way. Our faults contain a tremendous amount of energy. That energy can be used in a destructive or constructive way.

From this perspective, the more defects I have, the more ingredients I have. Anger, for example, can become one of our juiciest ingredients. If we have a tendency toward anger, we don't try to deny it or block it out. But we don't observe or analyze it either. We let our anger arise, so that we can feel anger fully. We sit with the anger. We *become* anger. When we do that we can see what anger is all about. Then anger will transform of itself—into determination, for example.

Once we acknowledge that anger is part of the meal we are preparing, we need to figure out how to cook a good meal using that particular ingredient. We can direct the energy of anger toward changing unjust social conditions, such as homelessness or racial discrimination.

For example, when we finished the building at 68 Warburton, our security system wasn't quite in place. The first thing that happened was that somebody broke into the superintendent's office and stole four gallons of paint and ten dollars. Then the childcare supplies, about a thousand dollars worth of donated toys, were stolen. At first the tenants were really angry. Everybody was enraged. And no one knew what to do.

When we called an emergency meeting of the tenants' organization, we found that by focusing on practical solutions, the anger slowly became transformed into determination. One tenant said, "Three years ago *I* was doing this kind of thing, and I think it's an inside job. So I think when this meeting breaks up, we should search every apartment in the building." Within one hour, all the apartments had been searched by the tenants. Somebody else said, "I've been coming in late and there are some people coming in and out of this building who look unsavory to me." Someone else said, "There's an intercom system to buzz people in and out, and I don't think we should be buzzing anybody in and out because who knows who's coming in behind them? I recommend we go out and bring in our guests." Everyone agreed. Someone else said, "We should create a tenants' patrol to try to catch who's doing this."

We had been having a difficult time getting the tenants to take more responsibility for running the building, but the anger triggered by the break-ins really galvanized them. It was their building, it was their space being violated, and they wanted to stop it. For a week or two, there were people up all night on shifts, watching things.

The break-ins made it very clear that the tenants wanted to take care of the building. Families who had no place to live for years now held in their hands the keys to their own apartments. They were not about to let anyone take that away from them. The building was becoming their home.

PROBLEM‑SOLVING

People think that the purpose of study is to get rid of delusion—or to bring us to a place of perfect understanding.

When we think there is a place where everything will be perfect and there will be no problems, we are living in the future. But the future is an illusion. We're always right here now. We think, and thoughts come up. We label those thoughts as relating to past, present, and future. But that thought of past, present, future is taking place now.

There will always be things coming up out of the blue. No matter how many techniques we learn, life will always be full of unexpected twists and turns.

This is a very basic point. It's true for anybody starting any endeavor. The typical problem with many managers, for example, is that they are looking for ways to get rid of all the problems—not realizing that a good manager is actually someone who knows how to deal with problems.

That's why there will always be the same amount to do. In fact, there will always be an infinity of things to do. We can never get our life or our business or our kitchen running exactly the way we want it to run. No matter how we envision it, it can't be that way. Life is not predetermined to the point that we can get to some stage and then see how it all works. What happens is that we have a better and better understanding of things, we have more and more clarity and ability to deal with things as they arise. But they keep arising, endlessly. The empty sky is always creating new clouds. The pot is always boiling.

According to the way of the Zen cook, Beginner's Mind has three basic ingredients. These three basic ingredients are doubt, faith, and determination. They're like air, water, and heat. You need all of them for every meal you cook.

Doubt is a state of openness and unknowing. It's a willingness to not be in charge, to not know what is going to happen next. The state of doubt allows us to explore things in an open and fresh way.

Like water, doubt is fluid. It has no fixed position. If you pour water into a round container, it becomes round, and if you pour water into a square container, it becomes square. In the same way, doubt or unknowing flows in accordance with the situation. It's the state of surrender, of being open to what is. Only when we raise sufficient doubt and questioning can we go further.

Our problem with doubt is that we take it to be a negative thing. We think that because we don't understand or because we are not sure, there is something wrong. When we get caught by the negative aspects of doubt, we wallow in self-pity. "How come I can't see it?" we say.

But this doubt can be positive. Positive doubt can allow us to see what this life is about. It can help us get rid of our complacency. By hanging on to what we know or understand and by being attached to a smug or complacent self, we remain stuck in a dead place.

But whatever we think we know is a trap. Everything we "know" pushes us to find ways to further whatever convictions we already hold or limits the range of what we might explore.

In the beginning, it's easier to experience our controlling mind, with all our attachments, than the open mind of doubt and unknowing. So the exercise is first to make a list of all our attachments. These might include ideas or things. You might, for example, list possessions you think you need, such as a certain kind of car or clothes. Then you might list ideas you consider important or true, such as the belief that you need to eat meat to get enough protein. The point is to lay bare all our attachments— everything we think is essential to who we are. Only when we let go of these attachments can we experience the open mind of doubt.

Another exercise that helps us raise doubt is the koan, "Who am I?" The question is designed to let you keep probing all the different concepts you have about yourself. Again, you make a list. You might start with your name: "I'm Bernie." But then you might think, "I'm not just Bernie. I'm an engineer." Then again, "I'm a father, or I'm a brother." And so on. But whoever you come up with is not who you are. It's one of the roles you play. But if you keep going, past all these roles and identities, you might eventually find yourself in a state of not knowing. That's the state of doubt we're talking about. It's breaking up this logjam of concepts, where we have so many ideas that nothing new is happening.

There are different ways to free ourselves

from the trap of knowing. In Zen, we use meditation to help us see that the trap is really made out of our concepts. If we're quiet and still, we can start seeing our concepts clearly, and start letting go of our attachments. This opens up the trap we've created for ourselves.

It's like the koan, "How do you go further from the top of a hundred-foot pole?" No matter how far we go in life, no matter what we understand or realize, we always stick to what we know at the top of that hundred-foot pole. This koan challenges us to go further, to leap into our doubt. That leap into the unknown allows us to see what it means to let go of the self.

Doubt leads directly to faith. When we let go of all concepts and ideas, we experience ourselves as we really are, not as an isolated individual but as part of an interconnected whole. This leads to faith in the oneness of life. It also gives us the faith to continue to let go of everything, including all our insights and spiritual attainments. Even though the path is endless, we keep going.

The third ingredient is determination. Even if you have doubt and faith, you need determination to take action. You might have an experience of the oneness of life, but without determination you could end up a vegetable. You might say, "The oneness of life—that's nice," and stay in bed, drinking beer and watching television.

Determination doesn't have to be extreme or dramatic. But when you apply the heat of determination, things happen. A chemical reaction starts—the water boils or turns to steam, the rice cooks, the bread rises. You get up early in the morning to practice meditation.

All three of these ingredients have to be present if you want to be a Zen cook. You could be very open and have a lot of faith, but if you have zero determination—if you feel that it's not the right time or you're not the right person—nothing will happen.

Actually, most of us have at least the minimum amount of these three ingredients we need to begin. Most of us have some doubt about who we really are or how we're living our lives. Most of us have some faith in the oneness of life—we believe that we all affect each others' lives or we know, from reading science, that we live in one interconnected biosphere. And most of us have enough determination to at least investigate different ways of resolving our doubts and deepening our faith.

In the beginning, it doesn't matter how much of these ingredients we have or what the proportions are. All that matters is that we have some amount of each. For the Zen cook, a seed of doubt, a pinch of faith, and a dollop of determination is enough to begin.

RECIPES FOR LIVELIHOOD

6
GREYSTON BAKERY

One of the early Zen masters, Pai-Chang, went out into the fields with his students every day, even though he was old and sick. His students tried to convince him not to work, but he refused. Finally, they hid Pai-Chang's hoe so that he couldn't work, but Pai-Chang simply said, "A day of no work is a day of no eating," and refused to eat until they returned his hoe.

THE MAIN COURSE

When we first moved from Los Angeles to New York, we were offered the chance to purchase a stately old mansion in Riverdale, an exclusive section of the Bronx.

At first, I didn't want to buy the building. We already had a small rented apartment that seemed sufficient. But a number of people, including my teacher, felt it would be a good idea. He liked the solidity of it and felt that it would help Zen get accepted in this country. Greyston, as the building was called, was set on two acres of beautifully landscaped land overlooking the Hudson River and the Palisades. Built in 1863 as a summer house for the Dodge family, it was constructed out of solid gray granite from a nearby quarry. It was designed by the renowned architect James Renwick, Jr., the architect of the Smithsonian Institute, Grace Church, and St. Patrick's Cathedral.

Of course, the solidity of Greyston Seminary was somewhat illusory. We had raised funds to buy the building, and then we supported ourselves by donations and fees from seminars and retreats. Many spiritual communities support themselves this way, but ever since the time of Pai-Chang, Zen Buddhists have emphasized the importance of work.

THE LIVELIHOOD COURSE

We don't live to eat. We eat to live. In the same way, our livelihood exists to support our life, not the other way around.

Livelihood is the course that sustains our body. It gives us physical self-sufficiency. It's the meat and potatoes, rice and beans, of the feast. It's certainly not the whole feast, or even necessarily the most important part, but without it we wouldn't have the strength or energy to prepare or enjoy the feast at all, either for ourselves or for others.

The main purpose of our livelihood is to sustain us. We need to make enough money to support ourselves and our family or community. We also need to make enough to put aside some reserves.

But in order to truly support and enrich our life, our livelihood has to be more than merely a way to make money. The livelihood course also has to include portions of all the other courses. When our livelihood lacks—or contradicts—our spirituality or study or social action, then we won't savor our work. When that's the case, we end up feeling malnourished or burnt out.

In the Buddhist tradition, right livelihood is the fifth spoke of the eightfold path taught by the Buddha:

right view, right intention, right speech, right action, right livelihood, right effort, right mindfulness, and right meditation. According to the Buddha, right livelihood should not harm others. Some people feel that right livelihood is livelihood that eliminates suffering completely. But every business causes *some* suffering or damage. This book, for example, has caused the death of trees. So right livelihood is livelihood that *minimizes* suffering or damage.

But for the Zen cook, right livelihood can also be much more than that. Right livelihood is the course that sustains *all* aspects of our life.

So right livelihood has to include a spiritual dimension. The spiritual aspect of right livelihood is that it helps us attain a transformation of consciousness from an ego-centered attachment to a recognition of interdependency, with each other and with the earth.

For example, many of the people who come to work at the bakery start out thinking only of themselves. To help them get a glimpse of the interdependence of life, we created teams that were paid according to how well each team produced. So if someone on the team didn't know the job very well, it behooved the rest of the team members to teach that person how to do the job better, because then they would all make more money. Working in teams helped to shift consciousness a little bit away from thinking just of how they were going to improve themselves. The focus was still connected with making more money, but now it functioned in terms of the whole group. This moved workers another step toward seeing their interdependence, which then allowed the next step to unfold, and the next, and the next.

Another aspect of right livelihood is that it

also has to include study and learning. It has to provide training in new skills and give us the opportunity to increase our knowledge.

And finally, right livelihood has to include social action of some kind. Right livelihood has to help or benefit others.

FINDING THE RIGHT LIVELIHOOD

It's not the business that makes right livelihood. It's the way we do business.

Some people know exactly what livelihood is right for them, or what kind of business they want to start. We didn't.

So we began by making a list of needs that our livelihood had to satisfy. This list gave us our recipe for right livelihood. Of course, because everybody's needs, ingredients, and tastes are different, everybody's recipe will be different. But many of the concerns will be similar. This was ours.

To begin with, we wanted a business we felt good about. As a Zen Buddhist community, we didn't want to engage in anything that fell outside the Buddhist definition of right livelihood. We didn't want to produce anything that would harm people.

In terms of spirituality, we needed a business that could be a vehicle for training, personal growth, and spiritual transformation.

In terms of sustainability, we needed a business that could be large enough to support a growing community.

In terms of study, we needed a business in which we could train Zen students with no experience in business. That meant we couldn't start a business that relied on highly trained professionals. We couldn't start a medical clinic, for example, or a law firm. (We had been able to run a medical clinic in Los Angeles because one of our community members was a doctor.)

In terms of social action, we needed a labor-intensive business that could create jobs for a lot of people.

And finally, we wanted a business in which we could excel. We wanted our products and our work to shine out in that particular field.

WHO YOU KNOW

Once we had determined our needs, we compiled a list of suitable businesses. We had about twenty-five possible businesses on our list.

The most obvious businesses on our list were ones we had started in Los Angeles. We had run a medical clinic, a construction company, a landscape company, and a publishing company. We also had some experience in housing—we had bought and renovated apartment buildings on a block adjacent to the Zen center. And then, of course, we had a lot of experience in what might be called the "business of Zen," which consisted of running a residential training program, retreats, workshops, and conferences.

But the obvious is only a place to start. We also looked at different businesses we could network with, especially businesses connected with other Zen communities. The San Francisco Zen Center was a natural networking possibility. They had a farm, Green Gulch, which grew organic vegetables, flowers, and herbs; a grocery where they sold their produce; and a first-class gourmet vegetarian restaurant, Greens, which was so popular you had to make dinner reservations months in advance. And they also ran the Tassajara Bread Bakery, which had grown out of the breads they baked for students and guests at the Tassajara Zen Mountain Center. In fact, *The Tassajara Bread Book*, which included many of their recipes, was a best-seller during the seventies.

We looked at many different possibilities. But we kept coming back to the bakery. For one thing, it seemed to be one of the most profitable of all the businesses we were considering. And it would also provide employment opportunities for unskilled workers.

But more than that, it just somehow felt right. It had a nice, warm, comfortable feeling about it. We also thought that it fit nicely with Zen. Baking bread, we told ourselves, was like growing rice in China. Rice or bread are both made from grains; they're both basic and they both feed people.

Baking also had another advantage. Bakers need many of the same qualities we were developing in our Zen practice: detailed care, mindfulness, meticulous attention, and harmonious interaction among all the persons involved.

WHAT YOU KNOW

It's important to realize that you don't have to know *anything*. It's more important to have the attitude of Beginner's Mind—a mind that is open and fresh—than to be an expert.

At the same time, it's also important to realize

that you can learn what you need to know from those who already know. We were fortunate to find another Zen community with experience in running a bakery. We were also fortunate that they were willing to share their experience with us.

But you don't have to stop if you can't think of like-minded people who can help you right away. You can ask friends, relatives, and acquaintances if they know anyone in the business you want to enter. If that doesn't work, you can find people and information by reading trade journals and going to trade shows and conventions. Most people love to talk shop because it gives them a chance to talk about what they know—especially if you're buying lunch.

SEE FOR YOURSELF

We sent four people to San Francisco for a month to learn how to bake and how to manage the business. That wasn't nearly enough time, of course, but because of the generosity of our friends at the Tassajara Bread Bakery, we were able to learn a great deal. When our team returned, we began to make our plans.

The San Francisco bakery was mostly a retail store and cafe. But New York was a very different environment, and we worked out a plan to open a retail store and go into the wholesale business. We figured out how much money we thought we'd require and how many people we needed to make a commitment. Six Zen students made a commitment to work for three years to get the bakery off the ground.

DETAILS ARE ALL THERE ARE

When you make a business plan, you have to look at the big picture. You have to know where you are going.

But you also have to know how you are going to get there. You have to look at the details. When we were remodeling the kitchen at the Zen Center in Los Angeles, Maezumi Roshi came in to ask how things were going. "It's almost finished," one of the carpenters said proudly. "All that's left are a few details."

Roshi looked shocked. "Details are all there are," he said.

Roshi has another way of saying the same thing: "A small thing is not small."

Business and marketing plans are always provisional, since life is always changing and no one can foresee all the variables. But a business plan without details is useless.

PAY ATTENTION

The greatest cause of failure comes not from lack of money, but from lack of attention. It comes from ignorance of what is taking place in your business.

Attention always brings us back to the present, to the details of any situation from moment to moment. Awareness, on the other hand, refers to a perception of the whole situation. Instead of paying attention to individual details, awareness takes a wider, more global perspective. Awareness is attention expanded to 360 degrees.

We spent a full year in preparation. This preparation took many forms: training bakers, researching equipment, researching market and sales, finding a bakery site, renovating the site, and most important, securing financial backing and the commitment of a core of Zen students.

KNOW YOUR COSTS

In order to run a business, you have to form an accurate picture of your costs. You have to know how much you will spend, and how much you will make. And you have to know *when.* You have to know when you need to pay your bills, and when you will receive money for your products. You have to understand timing.

You have to know what products make money and what products lose money. You have to take account of your indirect and hidden costs. You have to pay attention to the countless crucial details that make up the everyday life of your business.

When we made our business plan, we had to estimate the costs of our labor, supplies, equipment—walk-in freezers, commercial ovens, a dishwasher capable of scrubbing our muffin tins. We had to estimate the costs of rent, telephone, insurance, legal assistance, and packaging. In our marketing plan, we had to look at the advantages and disadvantages of selling retail or wholesale, or both.

It actually costs the same to run your business and your life. In both instances, you have to pay attention.

WHERE DID THE MONEY COME FROM?

This is one of the questions I get asked most frequently when I give talks about our work.

The answer is very simple. We borrowed it.

That's the way most new businesses get off

the ground. In our case, we borrowed it from one of our wealthier members. Banks won't lend money to new businesses. You have to convince somebody else—a friend, a relative, a venture capitalist—that the business will work. So of course you have to put in time doing research and marketing plans. When we began, we borrowed something like $300,000. At the time, it sounded like a lot of money. As it turned out, it wasn't nearly enough.

BREAD OR CAKE

When we first decided to open a bakery, we assumed that we would specialize in good, wholesome bread, which seemed like a very Zen thing to do.

But once I went to the Tassajara Bread Bakery and looked at their numbers more closely, I was surprised to discover that even though most people went to the bakery for bread, once they were there they couldn't resist the pastries. People didn't talk about it, but that's what happened. The biggest secret of the Tassajara Bread Bakery was that they made most of their money on the cake!

We were still attached to the idea of bread, though. What I liked best was something we called potato onion bread, which had real potatoes and onions in it. We also made the best challah I've ever eaten in my life, and I've eaten a lot of challah. We could sell as much as we made. And we did a delicious Swedish rye that was sold to the Russian Tea Room.

But there were problems with the bread business. Like most bakeries, we baked at night and delivered during the day. We had about thirty people living together at the Zen community in Riverdale, with maybe two-thirds of those working in the bakery and the rest working during the day at jobs outside the community. So the bakers worked at night, while the bakery drivers, salespeople, and office workers worked during the day, as did people with outside jobs.

We did our best to create a schedule where half of us were up all night and the other half were up all day. I thought in the beginning we could make it work, but it just wasn't healthy. It was dividing our community. Half of us were sleeping during the day, while the other half were working. Consequently, communication, which is the lifeblood of community, suffered.

We also found that if we marketed bread on a large scale, we would be competing with large chains like Pepperidge Farm. Gourmet pastries, however, were another matter, since they could be delivered to specialty stores. Pastries were also labor intensive, which was a drawback to many businesspeople but an advantage to us because it gave us a good opportunity for work-practice.

We began by experimenting in the Greyston kitchen during the night. We made brownies, goldies, coffee cakes, linzer torte, maple walnut cookies, and poppyseed cakes. People meditating in the morning would complain that the delicious smells interfered with the meditative concentration! And of course we had no shortage of people willing to taste our experiments.

And yet it's always true that you can't please everyone. No matter what you do, some people will be for and some against your plans. In our case, a number opposed our emphasis on pastries because they didn't consider it right livelihood. Some felt that cakes were harmful because they didn't fill basic nutritional needs, or because they used too much sugar, or because they were luxury items for the rich.

Of course, it's not always so easy to know what's right livelihood and what isn't. People have very different ideas about what's harmful. Many people who make weapons, for example, sincerely feel that they're helping to keep the peace. As for cakes, there's a large population that enjoys good cakes—including me—and I felt that if we could create the most delicious, healthiest cake possible, using real ingredients instead of harmful chemicals, then we'd be helping the cake-eating people.

BE WILLING TO EXPERIMENT

When we first started the bakery, everybody who worked there was a Zen student. As time went on, we would periodically hire somebody who wasn't a Zen student but who was a professional baker. It seemed that we had hit the limit of our experience and we needed someone who had knowledge we could learn from.

It was useful, of course, but one of the keys to our success, it turned out, was that we were amateurs. Since we really didn't have a thorough knowledge of baking, we experimented in nonprofessional ways. We tried things that normal bakers wouldn't even have thought of trying. We created some things that were unusual for the trade, and they made their mark.

We also took pride in the way our pastries looked and how they were packaged. This was a reflection of our Zen training, which in turn reflects Japanese ideals of beauty and harmony. The way food looks, the aesthetic element, is very important to the Japanese.

So our willingness to experiment and our

attention to how things looked gave us an edge. And because we were unique, people began to come to us.

When the people at Godiva Chocolatier hired a consultant to look for another baker, he found us. We baked for their Christmas catalog.

One of the most popular pastries we baked for them was their signature torte—a dense chocolate torte. We made it by modifying a recipe from the Tassajara Bread Bakery, and it turned out to be delicious and special. Around that time, we hired a professional baker to help us increase our efficiency—and he made a few changes in the way we prepared our Godiva chocolate torte.

Almost immediately, we got a call from the people at Godiva, and they said, "What's happened?" In fact, it was good. But it was good the way any other chocolate torte was good. It was no longer special.

We changed the recipe back to our original nonprofessional recipe and managed to retain the order. Experts can be useful, even necessary for certain tasks, but there's always a danger that they will turn your unique product into a professional thing that now competes with all the other professional things already out there. We had to learn to keep our uniqueness and style, even though every once in a while we did hire professional people to help us.

COOK FROM SCRATCH

In most bakeries nowadays everything comes in a mix. We open the box, and the instructions say to pour in a big pot and add five cups of water and cook for three minutes. Because of all the additives and preservatives and so on, it will always work, no matter what the conditions are.

But at Greyston Bakery, we make everything from scratch. We use real ingredients, with no preservatives, additives, or mixes. Most bakeries use a powdered egg mix, for example, because it's much cheaper and easier—you just add the amount of water it says on the box. But we use fresh eggs.

When we bake from scratch, we can't just add water according to the instructions on the box. We have to pay attention to all the conditions. It might be a hot day, there might be more humidity in the air, the flour might have slightly finer or coarser mill this time, the wheat might have been harvested at a different season. When we use ingredients like this, we have to teach people how to check every once in a while by tasting, by testing the texture, and so on.

When cooks learn to cook this way, they become real cooks. Unlike many bakers these days who only know how to use mixes, our bakers know how to work with the ingredients in all conditions, and so they can get jobs in the best restaurants and hotels.

Using ready-made mixes is like building up your life with ready-made wisdom, which is not authentic wisdom but just a set of handed-down assumptions. Ready-made wisdom, like ready-made mixes, might look like the real thing, but it won't be fresh, it won't really sustain you, and it won't taste as good. Most people who give you advice supply you with ready-made ingredients or tell you which ingredients to use.

Authentic wisdom, on the other hand, cuts away our conditioning so that we can come up with our own solutions. It helps us create a meal based on our own ingredients.

Meditation is a process that reveals our ingredients to us. So when people practice meditation, they are being led to find their own authentic wisdom. That's why, when people ask me for advice, I don't give them ready-made solutions, I always recommend meditation.

USE LOCAL INGREDIENTS

The bakers at the San Francisco Zen Center's Tassajara Bread Bakery very generously shared all their recipes with us. But when we came back to New York and actually started to bake, we found that we had to redo all the recipes, because most of the ingredients in New York were different from those in San Francisco. The water in New York, for example, was completely different from the water in San Francisco. The flour that we got from local mills was completely different from the flour in San Francisco.

Local ingredients fit local conditions and situations. They are almost always tastier and less expensive than ingredients trucked or flown in from afar. Buying local ingredients also supports and sustains our own communities and builds relationships. When something breaks, we know where to go. For all these reasons, the Zen cook always looks at what's growing in his or her own backyard first.

HOW TO SELL

We began our market research by looking in the phone book for prospective customers. We also read magazines and trade journals. We counted the number of health food and gourmet bakery shops within ten, twenty, thirty, forty, and fifty-mile radii from our base. Then we entered all the likely restaurants, gourmet shops, corporate food services, and department stores into our computer. Then somebody called each prospect to set up a sales visit.

Our first products were muffins, scones, and a few cakes. We began visiting stores in November 1982, to take advantage of the upcoming holiday season. Members with cars volunteered to drive our salespeople from one appointment to the next. We put our first samples in a nice red box with a lace doily. The first store we went to was Neiman Marcus in White Plains. They looked at the box and said it looked beautiful. Then they tasted it and said it tasted beautiful, and then they said, "We'll buy it." After that we went to Bloomingdale's, and they bought it too! The time of preparing and planning was over. We were in business.

A year or so later, by January 1983, we had forty-five accounts in Westchester and Manhattan. In August 1984, we added Macy's in Stamford and had a hundred customers, and our weekly sales were averaging $12,000 to $15,000, with about a quarter of that coming from a retail café we had started as well.

KNOW WHERE YOUR INGREDIENTS
COME FROM

It's important to know where our ingredients come from. We might think at first that they come from the wholesale supplier or the store—or that our water comes from the tap.

But the ingredients we use in our lives and

our livelihood consist of all the elements we're made of—earth, water, fire, air, and space. These elements are all interconnected, and each one has an effect on the others. The wheat ingredient, for example, includes soil, rain, rivers, and sunlight. It also includes the element of human labor and sweat—the farmers who grow the wheat, the workers who pick and pack it, the truckers, the processors, the packagers, the shippers, the advertising writers and designers, and the store clerks and cashiers who sell it.

When we see this, we realize that whatever we do, no matter how seemingly inconsequential, also has an effect on the environment, on our children, our grandchildren, and future generations. Dogen knew this very well. A river behind Eiheiji, the Zen temple he founded in Japan, contained an abundance of water. Mountain streams and waterfalls flowed into it. Nevertheless, when Dogen went to the stream, he would take a dipper of water and then put back half a dipper for future generations. That river is still called Half-Dipper River.

OUR SECRET INGREDIENT

Right livelihood is really at the heart of Zen, because of a "secret ingredient" that Zen Buddhists call "work-practice."

In Zen, sitting meditation, or *zazen,* is one way to practice, but it's not the only way. We can also meditate while we work.

In sitting meditation practice, we concentrate on our breath or a koan. In *samu* or work-practice, we concentrate on our work. If we are cutting grass, we just cut the grass. If we are washing the dishes, we just wash the dishes. And if we are entering data into a computer, we just enter data into the computer.

When we concentrate fully on our work in this way, there is no goal. We're not saying, "Oh, when is this work going to end?" or "I'm working to gain some money." We're simply working, fully present in the moment.

When we work in this way, we don't waste energy by worrying about all the things we should have done in the past or all the things we might do in the future. Rather, we use our work as a meditation practice that helps us stay in the present and aids our concentration. When we work in this way, instead of making us tired, our work actually gives us energy and peace of mind.

OUR MOST IMPORTANT INGREDIENT

Zen was probably the important ingredient in our cakes. But it was also the one ingredient that made many of our friends and advisors in the business world nervous. When we started the bakery, we wanted to call it "A Livelihood of the Zen Community of New York." We had a big debate about that. Most public relations people told us not to mention Zen at all because they were afraid that people would consider us a cult. They wanted us to call it the Hudson Valley Bakers, or Riverdale Bakers, or Better Breads, or Baker's Bounty. We had hundreds of names.

In the end, though, my response was that I didn't want to deal with people who didn't want to deal with us. I wanted people to know who we were. We decided to call ourselves Greyston Bakery, and we ended up putting the words "A Livelihood of the Zen Community of New York" right on the truck and on all the labels. A funny thing happened. It turned out that the public relations people were all wrong, because every story that was done about us—including those in the *Wall Street Journal,* the *New York Times,* and the Jane Pauley show—emphasized the Zen connection.

So it always works both ways. The bakery grew out of Zen and the idea of work-practice and right livelihood. But the publicity about the bakery also ended up defining Zen for hundreds of thousands of people who might never have heard of it before.

It's always best to be up front about who you are, and be frank about what you're doing. If people are uncomfortable with that, then you have a wonderful opportunity to communicate and work with people to alleviate their fears.

YES, BUT IS IT ZEN?

The truth is, you can't define Zen any more than you can define life itself. When people visit our community, and they see the bakery and the social action work, somebody always asks, "Yes, but is it Zen?"

"Yes, but is it Zen?" is a contemporary American version of a koan that appears in the classical Chinese text as "What is the Buddha?"

There's no right answer to that question. But all the authentic answers say the same thing. One of the famous answers, for example, is "The cypress tree in the garden." The Chinese Zen master Joshu answered,

"Three pounds of flax," because there happened to be three pounds of flax in front of him. If Joshu were working in the bakery today and someone asked him, "What is the Buddha?" I think he would respond differently. Probably he would look around him and say, "Three pounds of fudge!"

7
TIME AND MONEY

Time and money are both essential ingredients in the meal of our life. They are also inescapable ingredients. None of us can do without them.

Money and time are very similar in another way. People are always saying they don't have enough of them.

We all have different amounts of money, but we all have the same amount of time. We all have twenty-four hours in a day. And yet many of us feel we don't have enough time to do everything we need to do. In fact, the number of things that *could* be done are infinite, so if you think that you're going to do everything, or if you get too concerned about all the things you can't do, you're always going to feel you don't have enough time. In that case, time will control you.

Since there's a finite amount of time, it's really an issue of setting priorities and using the time you need to get certain things done that day. Then you are using time instead of being used by time.

If your plate is full, if you have this huge feast set out in front of you, then it's obvious that you can't do everything all at once. But this isn't a negative thing. It isn't a reason to feel overwhelmed or depressed. It's just that you can't eat everything on the table in one great gulp. All that means is that you have to make choices, which is what life is about.

There's always enough time. I may have only a small amount of time, but that shouldn't stop me from making my meal. Maybe I can only grab a snack. Maybe I will only be able to gather a few greens for a soup. It doesn't matter. You can always use the ingredients that are in front of you.

Just because you have a little doesn't mean you should do nothing. You can always do *something*. And doing something, starting something, making a gesture in some direction always enlarges the amount of time. The more you do, the more time you have.

How is this possible? When you get overwhelmed by all the things that need to be done, you end up spending all your time worrying about not having enough time. You can hear your mind ticking: "I don't have enough time! I can't get anything done."

If you feel overwhelmed, it just means that there's a lot going on, so time seems speeded up. If a business is growing, or if you're trying to end homelessness or free all the numberless sentient beings, then you're right. It *is* overwhelming. There *are* a lot of things to do.

But just because things are overwhelming doesn't mean that they have to overwhelm you. If you realize that things are not under your control, you can go step by step. You simply stop long enough to ask yourself, "What do I do with my time for the next hour?"

There's nothing very complicated about it. I make a list at the beginning of the day at work. I jot down different things I think I should get done that day and pick the ones I think are most important.

But I don't stick to my list slavishly. I'm not bound to it. If something comes up that's more important,

I'll do it. That's another way people end up feeling they don't have enough time. They make lists of what they have to do today, and then all of a sudden different things come up—like an earthquake! Forget your lists at that point and do what has to be done.

The key, as always, is to see clearly. How do we do this? The Zen cook always tries to set aside part of each day for a spiritual practice, such as meditation, which develops clarity.

When something new comes up, the Zen cook is able to make a choice about whether it has a higher priority. If it doesn't, you have to say, "Excuse me, I understand that . . . but what I'm doing right now is more important." The situation is always changing. If something can't be done today, I'll do it tomorrow, or the next day. It's always just step by step. One day at a time.

NOT ENOUGH TIME

One of the things I've found is that as I get to a place where there appears to be absolutely no more time, there's suddenly a tremendous amount of time. Just recently this year, I've been doing more than I've ever done before in my life. And yet I've found myself with so much more time that I began to develop other projects—a performing arts center and cafe in downtown Yonkers, an AIDS hospice, and an interfaith temple and seminary.

A Tibetan meditation master by the name of Dilgo Khyentse Rinpoche died recently in Bhutan at the age of eighty-four. He never slept more than three hours a night and devoted all the rest of his time to helping people. He was always available. He taught meditation, of course, but he also ran a big monastery that was really a school for Tibetan children and was involved in numerous other projects. He once said that his teacher didn't sleep at all! But you don't have to go to Tibet to see this sort of giving. The late Reb Schneerson, the Lubavitcher rabbi who lived in Brooklyn, also saw people all night. He slept for a few minutes in between.

These people are not superhuman. They're just people. But somehow they find that place where they can give all their time. And when that happens, you find that you have all the time you need. It seems that the more time we give, the more time there is.

How is this possible? Usually we function with a split between what we want to do and what we're actually doing, between what we wish we had and what we have. This division creates a loss of time and energy, and that loss actually wears us down. Since the mind wants something other than what's happening, it creates the delusion that there's not enough time or that time is running out.

But when we eliminate the gap between our expectations and what we're doing, our energies all go into what we're doing at the moment. We're not wasting our energy on what we think we should be doing. At that point, all of a sudden, the notion of time disappears. It's no longer a question of having not enough time or a lot of time. The very notion of time, of duration or interval, is gone.

The magic secret is to do just one thing at a time. We do what we're doing when we do it. It's just as my Zen teacher, Maezumi Roshi, told me when I first began to practice Zen: "When you walk, you walk." It's that simple and powerful.

NOT ENOUGH MONEY

Money is a very tricky ingredient. As with time, we usually think we don't have enough.

But how much is enough? How much money do we really need?

The Buddha didn't allow his monks to store things. There was no cushion or safety net. There were no refrigerators to save food or banks to save money. Every morning the monks had to get up, walk to the nearest village, and beg for food. Their existence depended on what they did each day. Each day they had to start over again, just to get their sustenance. They ate whatever they were given with an attitude of gratefulness.

Living that way gives each day real vitality. It makes you extremely active. It gets rid of complacency and allows you to function without fetters. I really believe that to be poor in that sense is the richest way we can live.

But that is not the same as living in poverty. When we live in poverty, we are always hungry—we feel we don't have enough food, clothing, or housing. On the other hand, when we live in luxury, we go through life feeling stuffed and bloated, as if we've overeaten.

The Zen cook avoids both these extremes by following the Middle Way of the Buddha. In terms of money, the Middle Way is free of the extremes of poverty and luxury. It is the way of sustainability. If we follow the principle of sustainability in our daily lives, we don't neglect our needs, and we are not greedy. We try to buy or create as much as we can use—no more and no less. We don't gorge or hoard. We shop for clothes to wear, not to put in the closet. We buy food to eat, not to sour and rot in the refrigerator. And we do our best to replenish what we use.

The Zen cook conducts business in the same way. One of the most innovative new management methods, for example, Just in Time Inventory (or JIT), makes use of the principles of sustainability. Businesses using JIT minimize their inventories. For example, we deliver the fudge brownies to Ben & Jerry's just as they are needed. That way you don't have to worry about food going bad or tying up huge fees for storage. Too much of anything creates problems.

The other side is that too little of anything can also create problems. When Ben & Jerry's lessened the amount of brownies they needed, we were forced to slow down our production. We had to go from two crews to one crew. A few months later, when they wanted more brownies, we had to add crew members again. This created havoc in our workforce. We've been discussing the problem with Ben & Jerry's and trying to come up with a system that works for both of us.

So we need reasonable reserves in both business and life. But that, too, is part of sustainability. Too little reserve creates anxiety and insecurity. But too much can dull the edge that sharpens creativity.

We also have the notion that we've got to have it all stored up, that we've got to have capital, savings, and insurance, and so we've created institutions solely for that purpose. Those things may be important, but when we get too caught up with them, it ruins the meal.

If we do find that we are making more money

than we need, it's time to enlarge the family we're feeding. That way we can always follow the Middle Way of sustainability. When Greyston Bakery began to sustain the Zen students who had started it, we began to look for a larger family to sustain. We started to train homeless and chronically unemployed folks.

The principle of replenishing what we use applies to businesses as well. When a business gives back to the community, it empowers the community to become self-sufficient. The result is that you have fewer people on welfare and more customers buying things. Both your company and every other company in the neighborhood will grow.

On the other hand, companies that just keep on depleting resources will be left without customers or employees and eventually go broke.

When we decided to get involved in social action in Yonkers, I felt it was impossible to do so while we were living in that rich mansion in Riverdale. So we put it up for sale. When you do koan practice, you try to experience things directly by becoming one with the situation. So I thought we would go onto the streets, with the people we were trying to help, to see the world through the eyes of the homeless, the underhoused, the unemployed.

As it turned out, we found a completely rundown house in the neighborhood. Ten of us moved in and did a complete rehab, which took six or seven months to finish. The basement was subdivided into a dormitory, and we took our meals communally. During this period we did our *zazen* as well as weekend retreats in the *zendo* above the bakery.

When we started our work in social action,

people said, "Well, how are you going to do that? We have a small community, and we don't have that kind of money. We don't have a million dollars." I said, "The problem is you're looking in your pockets. We have the whole universe."

As with time, there's almost always enough money to do *something*. When we looked at the money we had, for example, we found that there was only enough to produce a small thing. So that's what we did. We started working with the money we had. We baked bread for our local soup kitchen. You just start the process with whatever you have, and eventually the meal begins to take shape.

Suppose you don't have *any* money, but you have an idea of something you want to create. But if you sit around in your backyard and say, "I can't do anything because I have no money," who's going to join you? If you say, "Let's do something," it's amazing what can happen. People are attracted to action. You'll get joined by thousands of people from all over. People will want to see that idea realized, as a book or new kind of cookie or any product, for that matter, and money will come to it.

When we were beginning our work at Greyston, just sharing our vision attracted all kinds of help. Angelo Martinelli, a local politician, became a member of our board of directors. People from the Social Venture Network offered advice and contacts. Buddhists from other groups came to work with us. Government foundations made themselves available for funding.

All kinds of people wanted to become a part of it. As soon as they saw that we had not merely the vision but the determination to get things done—and that we had a history of getting things done—they knew we were not just dreamers.

JUST ENOUGH

Money is an absolutely necessary ingredient, but when it becomes the only driving force, when you focus exclusively on its accumulation, it can easily over-power and ruin a meal. Everything begins to taste sour.

When you're trying to help other people, though, you usually fall right into another kind of trap. You want everything to be nice. You're always worrying about doing good. The social action meal has a tendency to become too sweet. When that happens, the Zen cook adds the missing ingredient, which is wisdom.

If you want to do good but also want to have enough money to become self-sufficient, then you won't go too far in one direction. Money becomes an important lever, valve, or touchstone in social action—social action does the same with money. Both areas work in harmony. If your livelihood is just for money and has no aspect of caring for others, then you'll find yourself in the realm of the hungry ghosts. In the long run, your business will fall apart, because you're not giving anything back to the com-munity your money is coming from.

A LITTLE IS OFTEN ENOUGH

In some sense, the lack of money can be one of your best ingredients.

There is a famous story about a university professor who came to discuss Zen with a teacher. The teacher served him tea. And once the cup was full, the teacher kept pouring. "If your mind is full," the teacher said, "nothing new can enter."

If things are too full, it's hard for anything to happen. We hope that our approach to working with homelessness will serve as a model that can be replicated in other cities, including New York City. But the best place to create a model is a place where there is an absence of models—where there are many problems but not many solutions being tried.

It's like calligraphy. If you start off on a crowded canvas all full of marks, with lots of things going on, it's difficult to see the calligraphy. But the more space there is on the canvas, the more visible the stroke becomes. You can see the letters because of the empty space.

It's not a question of how much you have. You can make something very nice out of a few ingredients. In fact, when people start cooking, there's sometimes a tendency to throw everything into the pot—meat and potatoes and greens and all the different spices in the cupboard. But that approach doesn't work very well. It's too much. Everything cancels everything else out.

So it could be that a lack of ingredients has a certain advantage. The empty space can become part of the meal, too.

For example, because we did not have a mainstream background, government funding was not available to us at the beginning of our work. Not having the ingredient of government money turned out to be a big advantage. It forced us to develop our for-profit businesses and create a much more self-sufficient foundation on which to build our social work.

RECIPES FOR SOCIAL CHANGE

8
WHO ARE YOU COOKING FOR?

It's very important to remember that we have to take care of our own life. We have to cook for ourselves before we can really invite guests to join us for dinner. We have to nourish ourselves first.

A sick cook won't make a good meal, and a hungry cook won't wait for the meal to be served. If we don't begin by befriending ourselves, our meal will not taste right, no matter how hard we work, or how many ingredients we have, or how fancy our equipment is.

When we learn how to cook for ourselves, though, we find that our vision or understanding of the self grows and expands. The smell of food cooking and the warmth of the kitchen always invites people in. Even though it may seem as if we're cooking for ourselves, we're always cooking for everybody at the same time. This is because we are all interconnected. We are actually one body.

I sometimes use the analogy of one person with two hands. One hand is Sam, the left. The other is Bill, the right. Each has its own identity. When money arrives in the mail and Sam reaches for it, Bill gets a little jealous. When Bill burns himself on a hot stove, Sam thinks, "I should help him, but if I put the wrong kind of medicine on his hand maybe I'll get sued."

Eventually, they find that they have to work together to get anything done. Sam needs Bill to lift a heavy package, or drive a car, or even open a can of soup.

In this way, they discover that they are part of one body. They are one interdependent world. There is no more separation. When money comes, a hand reaches out, and it doesn't matter whether it's left or right. If a hand gets burned, there's no *thinking* about what to do, the other just automatically helps.

Of course, I don't say, "I have two hands." It's so obvious that I don't even say, "These are my hands." They're just part of me. I see you and me as separate until I realize that we are both part of one interconnected world as well. Eventually, all there is is one whole universe unfolding, and everything is taking care of everything else.

SELF AND OTHER

So the Zen cook cooks for others because he or she sees that the separation between self and other is illusory. This is actually very different from feeding others to help "them" or to do good.

My own interest in feeding others—in what people call social action—has a lot to do with what I can learn from the people I seem to be helping. By becoming one with them, by seeing the world as much as I can through their eyes, I learn what their needs are. At the same time, I broaden and expand my own view of life.

The social activists I most admire also learned from the people they worked with. A. T. Ariyaratne and his volunteers, for example, started a village self-help program in Sri Lanka called Sarvodaya Shramadana Sangamaya, based on Gandhi's work and Buddhist principles. "Sarvodaya" means "enlightenment for all," and "shramadana" means "sharing physical and mental energy."

The Sarvodaya movement empowers people to share their own mental and physical energy to solve problems and improve their lives without depending on government agencies or outside organizations run by "experts."

Ariyaratne began his work by going to an impoverished village, bringing people together, and asking the villagers what *they* felt they needed. The most important need, they all agreed, was for drinkable water. So Ariyaratne helped them to organize work teams to dig their own well. Everybody in the village contributed something to the common effort. Students went to Bangkok to find out about technology and materials. When a wealthy landowner volunteered to buy food for everyone on the work teams, the villagers discussed the matter and decided that most of them could share one meal a day with the volunteer workers instead.

When they had finished, they had not only learned how to dig a well that brought safe water to the village, they had also learned how to organize themselves to work together for a common goal. Once they had dug the well, the villagers found that they needed roads to get to the well—and so it went. Today Ariyaratne's Sarvodaya movement includes thousands of villages organized along the lines of self-sufficiency. Sarvodaya programs now include hospitals, schools, irrigation, farming, crafts, marketing, banking, and leadership training.

When we decided to build housing for the homeless, we wanted to help folks get off welfare. But when we went out to the welfare motels and talked to people, we found that most people wanted jobs but needed childcare first. Working together, we came up with a comprehensive model for the Greyston Family Inn, which included housing, childcare, counseling, and job training.

When we spent time living with the homeless on the streets, they told us that one of the biggest stumbling blocks to getting jobs or using available resources was not having any way to receive mail or telephone calls. So we began working with two homeless "organizers" to form the Greyston Retrieval Service. The organizers are working with homeless folks who live in different areas or "villages"—one village is a shantytown under the Brooklyn Bridge and another is in Harlem. The plan is for each homeless person to get a business card with their name, a mail address, and an 800-number voice mail box.

When we spoke to Ariyaratne about this idea, he said he would send organizers trained in the Sarvodaya movement to help with our work in New York City. Whether you're working in the third world in a Sri Lanka village or in the third world of America's inner city, the lessons of the Sarvodaya movement hold true: you can't go in with preconceived ideas of how to "fix up" the situation. You have to ask people what they need and empower them to find their own solutions. We need to change the world—and cook the meal—together.

WHAT ARE YOU WORKING FOR?

Recently a magazine in Westchester interviewed businesspeople to find out why they do the work they do. One percent said it was to improve the community or give back to the community. Seventy percent said it was to support their lifestyle. They didn't realize that if they didn't give back to their community, their lifestyle would fall apart.

The result is that there's very little housing in

Westchester for middle- or lower-income people. That, in turn, means that companies can't get workers, and communities can't get teachers or policemen or firemen, because none of them can afford to move to Westchester.

Of course more and more people are becoming aware that they have to pay attention to the communities around them. I recently spoke with someone at Digital Corporation, for example, who said that Digital *has* to be concerned about communities that are rotting away in order to prevent a loss of customers. Digital also realizes that by the year 2000 members of minorities will make up the majority of the labor force. If they're not educated well, and if they're not self-sufficient, then Digital's labor force will be in turmoil.

In one sense, this view is egocentric. But for Digital to grow internationally and become self-sufficient, it has to worry about areas of the world that are deprived because the people in those areas will not be good customers. So it's in Digital's self-interest to help those areas.

Spiritual self-sufficiency is similar. Most people think this involves building up a strong sense of self. But building oneself up—becoming the whole universe—really consists of what Dogen calls "forgetting the self." So we could say that the egoless state is really a vast ego state. It's a state where the ego is the whole universe. It's as if we become a point that has no dimension, but that point is the center of an all-encompassing circle. There's no longer any separation between us and everything else. At that point our concern about self-sufficiency becomes a concern that everything works together.

TEACH A HUNGRY MAN HOW TO FISH

When I first started doing this work, many students quoted that old adage of Lao Tse: "Instead of giving a hungry man a fish, teach him how to fish."

They felt that something was wrong with social action, that even if it was "politically correct," it wasn't "spiritually correct," because it offered people food instead of what was really important. They thought that as a teacher I should spend my time teaching people how to become enlightened.

I said, if I meet starving people, I first give them food. That's where they are. If I were hungry, I'd want to eat first. If I were homeless and cold, I'd want shelter. I wouldn't want to hear that there was a higher or deeper or broader range of whatever somebody else might think is spiritually correct.

That's not the point. The point is to identify with the people you're working with, in order to discover their needs. You can start working from there. Of course if someone is starving you don't just want to give him a fish. You want to teach him or her how to fish—which means you want to teach him or her how to cut a fishing pole, how to tie a line, how to use a hook, how to cast, and where to dig for worms. But you need to do all these things with the right timing. You need to start where people are.

9

GREYSTON FAMILY INN

We eventually found a location for our bakery in a low-rent, industrial warehouse district of Yonkers. Yonkers is just a few miles from Riverdale, but it's a very different world. Located only forty minutes by commuter train from New York City, downtown Yonkers is similar to many other neglected inner cities of America, except that it happens to be part of one of the wealthiest counties in this country. At that time, it was in the middle of a racially divisive fight over housing. The federal government had sued the city for not building affordable housing. It also had the highest per capita rate of homelessness in the United States.

From the bakery, we could look out onto the Hudson River and the Palisades. It was a beautiful view. But the buildings around us were for the most part run-down or abandoned.

As the bakery grew, we decided it was time to start making the transition from using the bakery not only to support ourselves but to help others as well. It was time to invite guests to the feast.

ONE MEAL A MONTH

Just at that point, we got a letter in the mail from a soup kitchen in Yonkers, run by the Sharing Community, saying that they had been serving three or four hundred meals at lunch, and they had run out of money. The timing was perfect.

We volunteered to take care of one meal a month. That meant we had to find the money, buy the food, and prepare a meal for three or four hundred people. We also began to donate bread and pastries, including some of our more creative experiments, to the soup kitchen.

Working with the soup kitchen made us aware of the different ingredients that went into homelessness in Yonkers. One ingredient was the city of Yonkers, which was all tied up in issues of integration and not doing anything. Still another ingredient was the style of homelessness: a large portion of the homeless population was made up of single-parent families.

A HOLISTIC APPROACH

At first it seemed that the easiest and most natural way for us to help would be to create jobs for the unemployed people in the neighborhood. It turned out to be more difficult than we thought. We took people who were unemployed and trained them as apprentices. Then we created a bakery training program in which a group of people attended classes half the day and worked on the bakery floor the other half. The program was funded by a city job-training grant.

During this period we began to learn how difficult it is to effect real social change if you look at only one element. In social action, as in making a meal or creating a full life, you always have to look at the whole picture. We found there was a critical need for counseling in what social workers call "life skills." We offered trainees drug and alcohol counseling as well as courses in basic communication skills, which gave them some idea of what to do if their bosses yelled at them or told them to do something they didn't like—instead of just stomping their feet and walking out of the building.

We were offering job training, but we found that many of the people who needed jobs didn't have housing or childcare. Many were living in motels. While a determined person could get to our program from the Yonkers Motel, the same person might be moved a week later to a motel in White Plains or even Connecticut, and that would be the end of his or her job training.

It was becoming obvious that job training alone wasn't the answer to unemployment. Sometimes if it was snowing or raining or a child got sick, parents would have to bring their children with them, and we would end up with kids running around upstairs. Without free or affordable childcare, we found it would be difficult if not impossible for single parents on welfare to find work.

But even if people had the time to look for work, they often could not find it. There weren't many employment opportunities in the inner city of Yonkers. So we had to think about the creation of jobs as well.

Later on we were able to design a program for people going to a culinary course run by the Yonkers high school system, which included both technical training *and* life skills. In some ways, just going to class for three months was important. People learned the value of work, what it meant to show up on time, and what resources were available if their kids got sick.

In the end, it seemed obvious that there was

no single solution to the problem of homelessness and unemployment. Our approach had to include housing, childcare, job training, counseling, and the creation of jobs all at once.

WORKING WITH BUREAUCRACIES

Bureaucracies tend to have written rules and regulations. So the first thing to do is to find out the ground rules. It doesn't matter whether or not you like them. It's just that if you want to work with a bureaucracy, such as a state housing agency, you need to follow its rules.

It's like the koan, "How do you go straight up a mountain with ninety-nine curves?" The answer is that you can't go against the curves. You go straight up the mountain by taking all the curves.

It also helps to remember that bureaucracies are driven by their budgets. You and they may both see the need for more money to fund a project, but budgets, like rules, are rocks in the water. It doesn't do any good to go directly against them.

Usually we think that we have to go through or over the rock that seems to be in our way. But the river never goes up against the rock directly. Water is gentle, but it is also the most persistent of the elements. It always finds a way to go around the rock.

In the same way we can always figure out another way around the rock. We can always find a way to work within the constraints. This may not be as difficult as it sometimes seems. You need to find the place where your goal—or some part of your goal—falls within the constraints set by the rules. You might not be able to get everything you need, but you might be able to get some part of it.

Sometimes it's as easy as redefining terms. The building at 68 Warburton was financed with money from a state housing agency that could not give money for childcare centers. But we were able to convince the bureaucrats who ran the agency that childcare was an essential part of the Greyston model. Even though the rules wouldn't permit it, they understood the need for childcare to make the housing work. Sympathetic bureaucrats figured out a way to help us fund the childcare facility by calling it a "recreation hall."

It's important to remember that every bureaucracy wants a program that works. After all, it needs to demonstrate that it's fulfilling its function. One success may give it a chance for more funding.

Even though you have to know and respect the rules, there are times when you can get around them. Keep an eye out for people of like mind who can help you navigate through red tape. Look for people who can make changes in the rules or who can tell you which rules are in the process of revision. Stay in touch with these people, even—or especially—when you don't have a specific need. Send them progress reports, photographs, press clippings, and releases. Invite them to informal social gatherings or other events where they can see (or taste!) your service or product.

THE BAKERY AS AN INGREDIENT

The bakery itself also turned out to be an important ingredient. For one thing, it began to provide us with enough of a basic livelihood so that we could help others. But it also provided us with confidence and respectability. Most businesses fail in the first five to seven years. But people knew that we had lasted a certain amount of time in business. They remembered that we had worked with some very established businesses—places like Bloomingdale's and Godiva Chocolatier. So when people saw what we had done, they felt they could trust us to deliver on the scale that we wanted to work at. They could trust us with large grants. They could rely on us to do the things we said we were going to do. We had good ideas, I think, but somebody else might have had the same good ideas and still not been able to project the kind of confidence we could. So the bakery turned out to be a very important resource in our social action work.

It worked the same way when I began to work with other community groups. People knew about the bakery, and they'd tasted our cakes. When I went to talk to Afro-American coalitions, for example, I was always introduced as "Bernie, the guy who makes all those great cakes." Then we could talk about politics and housing strategy and so on. I was still white, but I was more accepted because of my role in the bakery they all loved. And now we could open up. It happened over and over again.

All these—and more, of course—made up the ingredients of the meal we began to create, which took the form of our first building for the homeless.

It quickly became apparent to us that the usual approach to caring for the homeless—which was to house them in motels at great expense—was not working, and in fact could not work. Since the motels could make more money on weekends by renting rooms to prostitutes and their clients, they would routinely turn out homeless families on Fridays. Mothers or fathers didn't know where they would be when their children returned from the schools they were bussed to, and the kids whose parents weren't there to receive them after school would be taken into custody by the welfare agencies and often never returned. As a result, parents kept their children out of school. Single mothers or fathers couldn't rent apartments without money, and they couldn't get money without jobs, and they couldn't get jobs without training, and they couldn't get training without child care. Given this self-perpetuating cycle, it was hardly surprising that so many succumbed to despair and drugs.

FAST FOOD

Much of what passes for help is nothing more than a quick fix. You take, say, three thousand dollars and rent a motel room that puts a temporary roof over a person's head for a few nights. But the person is really being treated as garbage that has to be hidden away for a little while. Nothing in that money helps the person get out of the cycle.

It's like eating fast food instead of a real meal. You provide an immediate rush of sugar, which creates a hypoglycemic condition. Your physical state actually gets worse after a quick fix of fast food. You could, for example, take people into the country for three months and provide them with jobs, housing, and child care. But if they returned to the city after that time and there were no jobs, housing, or child care, they would be back in the same cycle.

THE COMPLETE MEAL

Most people could see that only a holistic, totally integrated approach could break the cycle of homelessness and poverty. We had to include all the elements and ingredients of a good meal. The biggest and most immediate problem, of course, was to provide some kind of stability, which for the homeless meant permanent housing. In order to do this we formed an entirely independent corporation with its own board of directors called Greyston Family Inn. Calling on some of the wealthy and influential people we met in Westchester, we began to work our way through the maze of red tape and bureaucracies until we finally obtained a grant from the New York State Housing Assistance Program to buy and renovate a deserted building a few blocks from the bakery, at 68 Warburton Avenue.

Usually, all the money earmarked for renovation goes to construction companies from outside the community. But this didn't make sense to us, particularly when there were so many able-bodied unemployed men and women in the community. So we formed a construction company, headed by minority managers and supervisors, that offered on-the-job training to unemployed and homeless people. Then we went to work, completely gutting and reconstructing the building. In this way, the money stayed in the community, and the homeless were involved from the very beginning in building their own homes as well as learning a trade. Finally, in October, two years after we had begun the process, the first eighteen families moved into their own building.

Once the building was completed, we began to add the other ingredients according to plan. Because the homeless were mainly single-parent families, we added a child care center. Because none of the parents had jobs, we added job training as well. We started a tenants' organization, encouraging people to take more and more control of running the building.

DRUGS

Everybody who moved into the building signed an agreement saying that they would not use drugs. Some people said we should test everybody for drugs before they moved into the building. But we felt that with the work we had already done, we had a good selection of folks, and that we would end up with a fairly stable building. Yet we knew drugs would be an issue no matter what. Given the environment we were working in, there was no way drugs were not going to be a major ingredient. After two or three months in the building, we guessed that out of eighteen families, maybe five individuals were still involved with drugs.

Quite a few tenants wanted the building to be free of drugs because they were worried about their own susceptibilities. They were in programs, like AA or NA (Narcotics Anonymous), and they were worried that they weren't strong enough to stay clean if people were using and selling drugs around them. At the same time, they said they didn't want anyone to know they had come to talk to us. They didn't want to break the code of the pack.

We approached the problem with a three-pronged attack. The bottom line was that we made it clear that we were not above making use of the police and the court system. We would be willing to go to court to evict people if they refused to work with their problems.

Second, we made it clear that we had the willingness and the resources to work with any family that wanted help. We brought in a team of drug counselors, who had been through programs themselves, to talk to the tenants about the entire family and the building as a whole. We also established links with various programs and groups. There is actually a lot of help for people who are ready for it.

And third, we created an intervention group of tenants who would talk as friends with people who had the same problems. This approach was probably the most important one, because it was in the hands of the tenants themselves.

10
BABY BUDDHAS

Homeless men and women are invisible to most of us because we have learned not to see them when we pass them on the street. But homeless children are really invisible because they are stuck safely out of sight in single rooms or motels.

Many of these children have suffered greatly, even before birth. Some have been beaten or sexually abused. Crack babies are born addicted, with damaged nervous systems. They are assaulted by violence as they grow up. One of our children had spent her whole life squeezed into a motel room with her father and brother. Late one night, a SWAT team, looking for a pusher who had cut up another drug dealer, descended on the motel, broke down the door next to her room, and rousted all the tenants, including her, into the hall. Naturally, she was terrified.

Taking care of these kids is absolutely necessary, both for their own sake and for the sake of their parents. Without proper child care, the parents cannot take the time to find jobs or get training. But this child care has to go way beyond "day care." These kids have been hurt, and they need real help. Without it, the cycle of neglect and violence will continue endlessly.

There is a famous Zen story about a teacher who was asked about the highest teaching of Zen. He wrote the word "Attention" on a blackboard. But isn't there anything else, he was asked. Yes, there is, he said, and he wrote the word "Attention" again. But there must be something more, insisted the student. Yes, there is, the teacher said. And he turned to the board and once more wrote: "Attention." Now the board said, "Attention. Attention. Attention."

That story describes the attitude of mind necessary for Zen study. It also describes the attitude needed to care for homeless kids.

Mitch Zucker spent most of his working day writing grants and development proposals for the Greyston Family Inn. But he also spent part of his weekend working with the kids.

Before the building opened, Mitch was helping out in a temporary day care facility we had set up while the parents were attending the Outreach classes. Just a few days before the classes began, we had all attended a lecture by a public health doctor describing the pathology of babies born addicted to drugs and alcohol. We were told the signs to look for and the behavior to expect.

Normally, Mitch's work involved being with the adults during the Outreach classes. But on the third day of the program, because of a logistics problem, we were severely understaffed in day care. As a result Mitch and one other person had to deal with twelve children, ranging from four months to eleven years, for several hours until reinforcements arrived.

As soon as Mitch entered the room, a three-year-old, perfectly matching the doctor's description of a crack baby, grabbed for him and wouldn't stop screaming until Mitch hugged him tightly. "He bonded like epoxy, latching onto my hip and refusing to let go," says Mitch.

"The moment I tried to set him down, he began screaming and thrashing, and the instant I hugged him, he stopped. This alternating scream-and-quiet behavior went on for almost an hour before I realized that the bond had to be more secure before I could care for the others.

"I tied him to my hip with a wide sash, then went about playing with the other children. It was like having a thoroughly benign but active growth on my left side. No matter how I bumped and jostled him while playing kickball, he remained placid. At one point he slipped down to my ankles almost upside down as I helped untangle a knot of screaming youngsters. It can work, I realized. All that's required is attention—lots and lots of attention."

Mitch worked with the kids every Saturday morning. He taught writing while another volunteer taught kids' karate to both boys and girls. The alternation of activity and quiet time seemed to work. "For me, it's all about homeless children, particularly those between six and eleven, the age-group I most enjoy playing with," he says. "For the most part, although I like their parents and have a feeling for their condition, I find them too self-conscious, too filled with anxiety to get to know them very intimately.

"But the kids show it and tell it like it is. We love each other's company, and I know the work we're doing is good for them. I've seen it so clearly that it makes me want to scream to grown-ups everywhere: 'Don't abandon the Baby Buddhas!' "

It's heartbreaking, but that's almost exactly what we have done. We have abandoned our children. When we first began looking for a building for our program, we found an abandoned schoolhouse that would have been perfect because it would have given us good child-care facilities as well as housing. But we soon found that agencies involved in housing wouldn't have anything to do with agencies involved in child care—and vice versa!

Remaining true to our vision, we insisted that we wanted a program that included all the aspects needed for self-sufficiency. What was needed, we insisted, were programs that included permanent affordable housing, preschool child care, after-school youth programs, job training, education, meaningful jobs, enrichment, and counseling—that was all!

In theory, at least, all of this is provided by our social welfare system. But often it is provided in a fragmented way that tends to lead to higher costs and bureaucratic inefficiencies.

There are many well-meaning and dedicated men and women in the various agencies and bureaucracies that provide social services. But many are trapped by the rigid structures of their organizations, as well as by competitiveness among bureaucracies for funding and status. Only a few are able to look at the whole picture. When we tried to put together a program that integrated all the necessary aspects, we found that nobody wanted to fund it because it was too "risky"—it depended on too many different agencies!

When we drew up plans for the building at 68 Warburton, we made child care a priority. We designed a full child-care facility on the first floor that included an office for a child-care director, classrooms and day care facilities, and a nursery for infants. The plans included a backyard playground, too.

Most low-income child-care facilities depend on federal and state grants. We had planned to use the Headstart Program. But we found that families who were employed would not be eligible after a one-year grace period. Headstart's restrictions would have made it more difficult for people to become self-sufficient.

We ended up running our own child-care program. The center was operated primarily for the families living in the building, but it was also open for other low-income families in the neighborhood. In addition, we started an after-school program for teenagers. The program was staffed by professionals. But we were also able to hire a few tenants as child-care aides. In this way, our child-care program filled a real need while contributing to the goal of self-sufficiency.

11

THAT AIN'T GARBAGE

A real Zen cook can make a beautiful offering out of ingredients most people would consider garbage. Soen Nakagawa Roshi, a contemporary Zen master, was famous for making use of things people had thrown away. He would go to the kitchen, pull things out of the garbage, and say, "This isn't garbage." And then he would show how to make a meal out of them.

He would go into Central Park, find a paper cup in the garbage, and pick up some leaves from the ground and perform a beautiful tea ceremony with that. Nowadays that might be a little risky, but the point is that he was able to make an elegant tea ceremony out of things that were thrown away.

I remember once, when we were preparing salads, one of our cooks was throwing the outer leaves of the lettuce into a big plastic bag. When I asked her why she was throwing the lettuce away, she said, "It's no good, we can't feed the people that." But those leaves were perfectly good. We used them to form the basis for a very nice salad.

When we were preparing meals for the soup kitchen once a month for three or four hundred people, most of the Zen students had very fixed ideas about food. They were preparing brown rice and other health-food meals that people didn't want to eat. We had to realize that the people who came to the soup kitchen had their own tastes and then figure out how to prepare nutritional meals that suited them.

PEOPLE AIN'T GARBAGE EITHER

It's the same with people. Our culture doesn't throw out only things—we throw out people as well. Homeless people can be seen as the "garbage" of our society. They're just discarded and rejected.

If you're homeless *and* you're HIV positive, for example, you can end up being rejected by the rejected. But just because someone is homeless, or because someone has AIDS, or is mentally handicapped or gay or black or white or old or whatever the reason doesn't mean that person is garbage. We all have something to offer. Whether you like them or not isn't the point. The point is to treat all offerings with dignity.

Many of the people who came to work in the bakery were rejected by the rest of society. They were not only unemployed, we were told, they were *unemployable.* They were not only untrained, we were told, they were *untrainable.* And now these "unemployable" and "untrainable" people are producing prize-winning cakes.

THE LOTUS IN THE MUDDY WATER

The pure lotus growing in muddy water is a metaphor for enlightenment. The lotus arises from all its impediments. It actually needs the impurity of the water for its nourishment. In the same way, in our own personal development, we can't just work with what we like about ourselves. We have to work with our muddy water. We have to work with our problems and hang-ups because that's where the action is.

Very few—if any—ingredients are garbage. Whatever work someone is doing is the feast that person is offering. Usually we don't see that because we are blinded by our own ideas of what the other person should be doing.

One of our best products literally came from an ingredient that almost got thrown away as "garbage."

A few years ago Ben Cohen of Ben & Jerry's and Anita Roddick of The Body Shop and some other socially conscious businesspeople went down to the Amazon rain forest to see if they could find products that would help preserve the rain forest instead of destroying it in the way that logging, cattle farming, and gold mining were doing. They were looking for ways both to help the indigenous people who lived there and to make rain forest preservation economically profitable.

Anita Roddick found a number of herbs and oils that could be used in her body care shops. Ben decided to make and market a candy called Rain Forest Crunch using brazil nuts. To do this, he formed a new company that would allow him to give away all his profits.

Ben came up with the recipe for Rain Forest Crunch candy in his kitchen. After he began marketing it, he realized that he was throwing away large amounts of "dust" that resulted from grinding the brazil nuts. But that "dust," he thought, could actually be used as a flour to make cookies, and so he went back to his kitchen and came up with the Rain Forest Crunch Cookie. Then he came to us and asked us if we would be interested in baking the cookies, which would be distributed by his new company. People come to us with new ideas for cookies all the time, and usually we're not interested. But there were three good reasons for baking Ben's Rain Forest Crunch Cookie. First, the cookies were helping to save the rain forest. Second, it was new business for us. And third, we wanted to work with other companies, like Ben & Jerry's and Ben's Community Products, who were strengthening the idea of business as a force for social change.

We're now working on exporting the Rain Forest Crunch Cookies to Japan. It's difficult, because we have to meet Japanese agricultural standards, but we've been working with a firm in Oregon that tests products for the Japanese market and are making good progress. We also need very good packaging. It has to be not only aesthetically appealing but strong enough to protect cookies, which are very fragile.

So far we've come up with a tin that can be reused as a container and a small bag that can be sold to airlines. Each cookie is individually cushioned in its own plastic container. We've put it through extensive testing. We throw the tins and packages down the stairs a couple of times, and then open them to see the results.

We expect that the Japanese will take a million dollars' worth of cookies a year. In addition, the boxes contain a beautiful representation of the rain forest and written information explaining the ideas of sustainable development, which will help educate the Japanese public on rain forest issues. Not bad for a product that began as "garbage."

12

THE MEAL OF SELF-SUFFICIENCY

At the first tenants' meeting before our first Thanksgiving someone asked, "What is Greyston Family Inn going to do for us for Thanksgiving?"

The question was a natural one for a person still in a state of welfare dependency, in which people give you a lot of stuff, relatively speaking, a few times a year on special holidays. So I just countered, "Yeah, what are you going to do for Thanksgiving? Because," I said, "you're in Greyston Family Inn now, and you're in charge."

The person who had asked the question was stopped. Then I went on, "One of the things I thought might be nice would be for you guys to throw a party, a Thanksgiving dinner for your friends who are still in the motels."

The tenants were shocked by my suggestion. They said, "No way! We're not going to do that. Those people are druggies. We'll have a bad Thanksgiving. We won't be able to get them out of the building. We want to leave all that behind."

I said, "You must still have some friends left in the motels or on the streets."

"Nope," they said. "None of those people are our friends. Not anymore."

And another woman said, "I don't want a big party. I want to have Thanksgiving just with my family." She was the same woman who had brought up the question of Thanksgiving in the first place. She was a grandmother who had become homeless when her daughter gave birth to a baby at the age of thirteen. Her daughter had taken off, and when the grandmother quit her job to take care of her grandchild, she lost her apartment and became homeless. Her desire to have Thanksgiving just with her family made sense.

The tenants' unwillingness to share their new home with the people still in the motels might seem ungenerous, but it was a positive sign at that time. They were realistic enough to recognize how important it is to have some measure of security and self-sufficiency before you can begin to help others.

From the very beginning, the mission of Greyston Family Inn was to help homeless families from Yonkers who wanted to become self-sufficient and get off welfare. The meal we offered consisted of a specific program, which we made as clear as we could—it was written out in the menu, so to speak—so that everybody involved in the program knew what they were getting into.

Of course, we couldn't force people to follow the Greyston program. Since we were offering permanent housing, once people moved in it was up to them what they did in their homes and with their lives. But we did do our best to select people who wanted the meal we had to offer.

We began by inviting homeless people living in the motels around Yonkers to a meeting, where I spoke about the Greyston Family Inn program, asked them about themselves, answered questions, and left applications for weekly classes.

We started running two classes, morning and afternoon, every Saturday. Each class had about twenty people. We provided child care during the classes, but the students still had to gather up their kids on Saturday and get to the bus, which we also provided, on time. Just getting to the classes was actually a key element in selecting people for the program. So was regular attendance.

The first sessions dealt with building up dignity and self-respect. Then we started to explore issues of communication and group interactions. We played games and did exercises that demonstrated the value of operating together as a group instead of independently. We also did some testing and tutoring in basic skills.

We tried to make it clear to everyone that the building would not be a shelter or a soup kitchen. It would be permanent housing. And we talked about our hope that people would eventually be able to own their apartments.

Making the transition from the welfare mode to self-sufficiency is not easy. As dehumanizing as the welfare system is, it provides certain basics: a soup kitchen, space in a motel, shopping bags full of gifts at Thanksgiving and Christmas. It's like eating a huge amount of sugar, which is addictive: as soon as you finish it, you need more. With certain expectations of what's going to be given to you, you can lose hope and the ability to go out and change things.

So people have to believe that they can change themselves and do something in the world around them. Only when they feel secure helping themselves can they begin helping others.

I wanted to make sure people understood they might be more comfortable where they presently were, because they already had housing, a soup kitchen, and certain things given to them, whereas in our building, they'd be in charge of their own lives and would have to make their own food, keep their own kitchens, and take care of all the hassles that come with self-sufficiency. And so a number of people who didn't want to experience the hassles of our intensive program let themselves out of the program by not showing up.

Drugs were also an important issue. Every potential tenant went through an assessment by a drug counselor, and some people who seemed unstable in that area were not selected. A few families seemed to fall into the category called "weekend warriors"—people who were into recreational drugs. But like everybody else who planned to move into the building, they signed a statement saying, "I understand the use of drugs is not allowed in this building and is cause for eviction." And they signed a contract in which they agreed to be tested for drugs at any time.

When we had our midterm graduation, the groups had dwindled to about ten students each from an initial twenty in each class. We combined these two classes into one class that met every Saturday for five or six hours. At the end of eight months, we were down to sixteen families out of twenty. We chose twelve from those sixteen because we felt that four of the families were still too unstable and risky. Then we got a grant from another agency for another organization, called Project Self-Sufficiency, to run a similar program for another group every day for a month, and we selected four more families from that group.

We had our final graduation in a school auditorium. We made up certificates: "Success on Completion of Greyston Family Inn Course." It was a real ceremony. People invited their families and friends. We had some local celebrities there. And the graduates were flabbergasted. Most of them had never gotten a certificate for anything in their lives.

CHANCE AND CHOICE

When it came time for people to move into the building, we continued to stress the principles of choice and individual responsibility. Nothing was simply given.

In order to offer a way for the new tenants to furnish their own apartments with dignity, we created a kind of lottery in which the order of choice was set by chance but the choices within that order were left completely to the tenants. The family that pulled "1" out of a hat got to select one piece of furniture first. The family that picked "2" got to pick one piece of furniture next, and so on. They could pick a color TV or a big kitchen table. It was up to them to figure out their priorities and how those priorities fit into their budgets. They couldn't blame anybody else. While all the tenants had the same constraints, they were also all making their own choices.

Usually, when homeless people move into housing, they are given either furniture or a furniture chit, used much like food stamps, by a social services department. If they are given furniture, of course, they are denied any choice about how to furnish their apartment. And if they are given a furniture chit of two or three hundred dollars, they have no other choice but to shop in the stores that sell schlock furniture.

So we assembled a decent collection of furniture by soliciting donations from individuals and groups.

Pieces were priced so that families could furnish a whole apartment within their allotment. The remaining chits were used to buy furniture for the common areas. In this way, furnishing the apartments became an exercise in self-sufficiency and self-esteem.

TENANTS AS LEADERS

Once people had moved into the building, the tenants' organization became the focal point for developing self-sufficiency and community through conflict resolution, family support, and social activities. It met regularly to discuss maintenance and management of the building, to learn about leases and tenants' rights, and to become involved with the financial responsibility leading to equity ownership in the building.

In the beginning, the weekly meetings were run by a tenant organizer who trained the tenants to run the meetings themselves. As time went on, the tenants took over more of the leadership themselves. They elected a chairperson, a secretary, and a treasurer. They learned Robert's Rules of Order. They formed committees. And they began to develop trust, both in themselves and in each other.

"I finally realized what drugs and alcohol had done to my life," one tenant says. "I realized that I wasn't bad, but I was sick and needed help. That took a while to sink in. For a while, things at Greyston were going against my grain. It was frightening. But I ended up enjoying life here, and it made me believe that I could do things I never thought I could do. Not only that, other people began to believe in me. Can you imagine me being elected the treasurer of the tenants' organization? I never had a bank account except for a few months about ten years ago. But now I'm learning fast and loving it."

FROM HOMELESSNESS TO HOME OWNERSHIP

Because we are committed to self-sufficiency, we do not offer handouts, welfare, or temporary housing. We offer all the tenants at 68 Warburton the chance to buy their apartments at a very good price.

But that's very hard for tenants to envision. Right now they all pay a third of their income toward rent, and the federal and state governments pick up the rest. The rent value is set by the government as a fair market value for the area.

It's a very slow process. Having a key to your own apartment is a tremendous first step—but it's still only a first step. People need time to recover from homelessness just as people need time to recover from drugs or alcohol. There is a lot to assimilate when they haven't dealt with banks, telephone companies, or public service for years, if at all.

In order to be eligible to buy their apartments, tenants have to become active members of the tenants' association, taking responsibility for setting the rules and regulations for the entire building. The tenants' association has a number of committees, including a security committee and a committee to set up a revolving emergency loan fund to help families pay their electricity bills. There are also certain rewards and perks. Members of the tenants' association may use the common room for parties and can borrow the TV and VCR.

We also offer a number of counseling and

training programs. There are life-skills classes to help people look for jobs and classes on family wellness. Many of the tenants attend drug or alcohol programs as well.

It's important to keep a dialogue going to find out what people actually need and want and can handle. Some people feel that the more programs, the better. But you have to be careful. If too much is going on, people feel overwhelmed and overloaded. Then you reach a point of diminishing returns. You can't impose your ideas. But at the same time you have to make good programs available.

So far the results of the program have far exceeded our expectations. One tenant had a job when people began to move into the building—and he lost it almost immediately, partly due to the pressures of being reunited with his wife and kids. But within five months, eleven out of twenty-five adults in the building were working. Four were employed as child-care aides in the building, and some were planning to get further training to become assistant teachers and then teachers. One person was working in the bakery, another as the superintendent of the building. And the rest had jobs outside. Six were completing high school equivalency courses. One was studying radiology in college, and three completed a beginning word processing course taught by Greyston Family Inn and were enrolled in a more advanced course in a local education center.

But the greatest change, perhaps, is the change from despair to hopefulness. As one tenant says, "Besides everything else—besides the apartment, child care, and job help—the one thing Greyston offers is encouragement. After you're homeless a while, once you feel you're alone, it takes its toll on your self-esteem. You look at yourself the same way the public looks at someone who's homeless: as someone who can offer the community nothing."

Another tenant, who came to Greyston along with her newborn child and husband after two years of homelessness and unemployment, sums it up this way: "At this time last year," she says, "if someone came and told me I would have a beautiful apartment, and I would have day care, and I would be able to go to school and, hopefully, within six months get a job, I wouldn't have believed them—because I've never seen anyone who was homeless and ever came out of it. But I'm doing it. I'm not successful yet, but I will be—I know I will."

Such progress is wonderfully heartening. But every up has a down; every success creates more "problems." The meal served at the Greyston Family Inn is a very rich one. Even though we've been successful, we have to be careful that people don't get sick from eating too much too fast. There has to be enough time to chew and digest all the new information and experience. Recovering from homelessness, we've learned, doesn't happen overnight. It's an ongoing process.

RECIPES FOR COMMUNITY

One of the key principles of the Zen cook is that nothing exists by itself. Everything is interdependent.

Even though we all have responsibility for our own life and work, at the same time none of us can accomplish the work we need to do all by ourselves. This is especially true if we want to help others. We all need to work together to prepare the supreme meal.

The Zen cook's way of working with others is based on the vision of Indra's net, which is the Zen model of life. Indra was an ancient king of India who thought a great deal of himself. One day he went to the royal architect and said that he wanted to leave a monument of himself—something that all people would appreciate.

The king's architect created an immense net that extended throughout all space and time. And the king's treasurer placed a bright, shining pearl at each node of the net so that every pearl was reflected in every other pearl. And each single pearl—each person, each event—contains the whole of Indra's net, including all of space and time.

When we realize that we are all bright pearls in Indra's net, we see that within each one of us the whole body of the universe is contained. Since we are all already connected in Indra's net, there are no limits to the possibilities of connecting with other people in our lives and our work.

Still, it's natural for most of us to begin "networking" with the people closest to our own interests and needs. Accountants network with other accountants, poets with other poets, and Buddhists with other Buddhists. This kind of networking certainly has its uses. It's especially effective, for example, when we need help in solving a very difficult problem. But it is not a very effective overall strategy, because it leads to a narrowing instead of a widening of your network. It results in ever-diminishing returns. The tax accountants end up talking only to other tax accountants; the free-verse poets end up talking only to other free-verse poets; and the Zen Buddhists of one school end up talking only to Zen Buddhists of the same school.

When we network according to the vision of Indra's net, on the other hand, we begin by casting the widest possible net. We do this by defining our mission in the broadest possible way. If I define myself in the narrowest sense, for example, as a Zen Buddhist monk who is involved in running a bakery and providing housing for homeless people, I might limit my network to Zen Buddhists, bakers, and social workers.

But I can also define my mission—or vow, to use the Zen Buddhist term—in a much broader way. I can say, for example, that my mission is to prepare the supreme meal for the benefit of all sentient beings. I am now casting a much wider net—an immense net, in fact— for I can now work with anyone who wants to improve the quality of life on this planet. (Of course, as you define the specific issues and ways in which you want to work, you will naturally find yourself working with a particular segment of the net. But even then—*especially* then—it's important to remember you're still part of a bigger net.)

When we network in this way, according to the vision of Indra's net, we will naturally end up including all kinds of different people. When we put together the board of directors for the Greyston Family Inn, we looked for the widest possible participation from the Yonkers community. Because we cast such a wide net, we were able to include two former mayors of Yonkers, Al DelBello and Angelo Martinelli. Angelo was a Republican and Al a Democrat, and they had run against each other more than once in the past. In fact, one campaign had involved a certain amount of mudslinging. But both were committed to improving the quality of life in Yonkers, and both could see that we were trying to do the same thing. And of course they were both part of different networks. Their connections extended from the city to the county to the state and made it much easier for us to get things done. When there was a delay, or when something went wrong, we could always count on either Al or Angelo's knowing the right person to call.

Each of us also has people who don't want to work with us. But we can look at this as a kind of negative network. People who wouldn't work with us might be willing to work with Al, people who wouldn't work with Al might be willing to work with Angelo, and so on. So by networking with Al and Angelo—or with any two people who represent different points of view—we didn't just double our network, we quadrupled it.

DON'T WORRY ABOUT COMPETITION

All too often we view other people in our field—whether it's business, social action, or even spirituality—as rivals or competitors. We seem to feel that there are only so many resources to go around, and that if someone else is doing well there will be less for us.

Actually, the very opposite is often the case. Rivals are often allies in disguise. When we give up our own agendas and fears and identify ourselves with our "opponents," we find that we have much to give each other because we can each supply an ingredient or point of view that the other is missing.

The world is so vast and there's so much to be done that it doesn't make sense to worry about competitors. It's like a feast. You don't have to be afraid that the other guests are going to eat all the food.

It makes more sense, I think, to welcome competitors as guests and try to transform them into allies we can work with and learn from. When people call and want to know what I'm doing, I'm always open with them. This is because we *want* other people to do what we're doing. We want other people to copy us and replicate our models.

We've hired other people even though we knew they were planning to start similar bakeries of their own. We helped the Trappist monks of Snowmass start their own line of cookies. We even published a cookbook, *The Greyston Bakery Cookbook*, with all the recipes for our unique gourmet specialties. Once we did that, we didn't have to worry about anyone stealing our recipes!

Another problem with competition is that it breeds secrecy, and secrecy creates both an unhealthy state of mind—paranoia—and an unhealthy industry of corporate spies. If you use spies, you always have to worry about double agents who spy both ways, and that weakens your internal organization. But if everything is out in the open, if you have no secrets to steal, then you can concentrate on sharing information and creating cooperation within your company. Instead of sowing seeds of suspicion, you will plant the seeds of harmony and strength.

Secrecy may seem better for the short term, but it doesn't open the way for growth in the future.

NETWORKING IN

It doesn't work to just network out. You also have to find the right people to work with in business or social action. You have to know how to network in.

If you are running a large organization, it is especially important to know how to select managers you can work with. There are two basic criteria. First, you need someone who has the skills needed to do the job. And second, the manager must be able to actualize the vision that drives your enterprise. This does not mean that the manager must have exactly the same vision that you have. Indeed, that is highly unlikely, since we are all unique individuals. It is enough that your vision and the manager's vision dovetail.

It's worth taking your time to find such a person. I spent two years talking with many capable people before I found Jef Hoeberichts, who became the general manager for Greyston Bakery. Jef started working for us as a business consultant. He had little interest in Zen. But he was passionately interested in creating self-directed management teams at all levels of business. And his vision dovetailed nicely with our vision of creating self-sufficiency.

Because of this I could leave Jef alone to solve

day-to-day problems and generally run the business in his own way, and he could work freely without having his creativity blocked by having to second-guess me all the time. Even though we might not have exactly the same vision, we could work together in an atmosphere of trust and mutual respect.

14

SOCIALLY CONSCIOUS
CONFECTIONERS

In 1987 a group of "socially conscious" businesspeople held a conference at Gold Lake, Colorado. At that time there were a number of funds and investment groups that wouldn't put their money into companies they felt were violating social and environmental ethics. But there weren't many funds or companies actively supporting good causes. They would just say, we won't give you any money because you discriminate against women, or you invest in South Africa, or you make bombs. It was mostly a negative approach. So one of the ideas of this conference—which was the beginning of an organization that's now called the Social Venture Network—was to find ways to fund groups that were doing good work.

The first day I arrived at Gold Lake I met these three guys, Ben, Jerry, and Jeff. Ben and Jerry had started an ice-cream company in Vermont, and when it began to get successful, they brought in a friend of theirs, Jeff, who did accounting and legal work.

Ben and I took a walk around Gold Lake and began to talk about what we were each trying to do. We had a lot in common. We were both part of an elite group of what I like to call "socially conscious confectioners." We were both from Brooklyn. We also had something else in common. My family didn't have a lot of money when I was growing up, so I started working pretty early. And one of the jobs I had was selling ice cream on the beach during the summer.

But we were also coming from different directions. Ben thought of himself as a businessman reaching toward spirituality. He saw me as a spiritual person reaching toward business. Actually, I think we're both more like socially conscious entrepreneurs than purely businessmen. Ben recently told me that the blessing and curse of the entrepreneur is to see opportunities everywhere. There are opportunities everywhere because the world is full of needs. Whereas some people panic when they see those needs, an entrepreneur says, "Great, that's an opportunity to do something."

Some socially conscious businesspeople donate part of their profits to help various good causes. There's nothing wrong with that approach, but both Ben and I prefer to do business in such a way that it brings about social change directly. What makes a company like the Greyston Bakery and Ben & Jerry's and several others stand out is that the notion of social action is integrated into the company structure.

When your model is to create money to fund something else, then your driving force is money. It's not social action. You may take a percentage off the top and donate it to various worthy causes, but your business is still being driven by the money motive. We started out that way, but now we have shifted from being a company that makes money to donate to causes to being a company that creates jobs and engages in community development.

It's much more direct and effective to use your resources to create the best environment to accomplish your vision.

After we had circled the lake a few times, Ben and I began to talk about how we could work together. Ben & Jerry's has a number of franchises around the country. Our first idea was for us to sell our cakes through the franchises. But our cakes needed refrigeration, and Ben & Jerry's didn't have any refrigerated display cases for cakes in their stores. They would have had to redesign their stores or we would have had to make cakes that didn't require refrigeration.

The next time we met was at the Omega Institute in New York. Ben and I and Bob Schwartz, the founder of the Tarrytown Conference Center, were doing a workshop for people interested in making their business or working life more socially responsible. Ben was very interested in using socially responsible suppliers. He figured that by buying products from people who were socially responsible he would support their business and create a network that could bring others in.

As it turned out, Ben was having a problem with one particular ingredient. It was a chocolate fudge brownie wafer, which he was using to make ice-cream sandwiches. You take two of these wafers, place a dollop of vanilla ice cream in between, and you end up with a chocolate fudge brownie sandwich.

At that time, Ben & Jerry's was buying millions of dollars' worth of this wafer from a bakery in the Boston area. His dependence on this one vendor, which might go out of business or raise prices, made him nervous. So in the interest of good business, he wanted a second vendor, and in the interest of social action, he thought of us.

But since the new bakery was going to serve as

the second vendor for a given product, the second bakery's brownie wafer had to taste identical to the first. Ben had tried for two years to find another bakery to make that wafer.

Since the Boston bakery was not willing to share its secret recipe for the fudge brownie wafer, we would have to develop a process and a recipe for a fudge brownie that would be an identical match to the first one. And that meant that it had to match *after* you put the ice cream between it, froze it (which was when the ice cream got absorbed into the wafer), and then defrosted it to eat.

At first we were leery about going after this contract, because it was very different from our usual line of business. We were making fancy cakes and tortes. We were making custom-made cakes, from prize-winning cheesecakes to artistic pastries.

But the wafer, though it had to be of the highest quality, was a mass-produced item. And of course we would need quite a bit of money to buy the new equipment and supplies and to train new workers. (In fact, we wound up needing $500,000.)

Then there was the problem of duplicating the brownie itself. Instead of donating money to us, Ben gave us the contract to make the chocolate fudge brownies for his Chocolate Fudge Brownie Ice Cream. Making that many chocolate fudge brownies was very different from the labor-intensive, prize-winning cheesecake and other custom-made pastries we had based our reputation on. But it substantially increased our business and allowed us to hire a whole new crew of our neighbors as workers and to train them in a trade that would make them self-sufficient. And it gave us the chance to work with another socially conscious business in a way that could potentially help both our businesses.

So without any experience in this kind of large-scale baking, we set out to match the other company's secret recipe, spending weeks experimenting with our batter to get the taste and consistency just right. We kept sending batches of it up to Ben & Jerry's plant in Vermont, where it was subjected to blind tasting tests.

Finally we were told that while our chocolate fudge brownies did not match the other company's exactly, they were close enough. We got the go-ahead, hired and trained a crew, and invested heavily in expensive automatic mixers and ovens.

Then disaster struck. Ben & Jerry's quality control people decided that the match wasn't close enough after all and canceled our order. And when that happened, the bank that had given us a letter of credit based on our order from Ben & Jerry's demanded that we give up our work with Ben & Jerry's and go back to our cake and cookie business. They wanted us to cut our losses. In fact, the bankers told us that if we didn't do this, they would cancel our line of credit *and* call back all their loans—which came to over a hundred and fifty thousand dollars that we didn't have.

We could have decided that we'd failed then and there and closed the bakery. We could have said that since we hadn't gotten it right, we ought to give up. But to my way of thinking, it was not a matter of doing something right so much as doing something to the best of our ability. We wanted to work with Ben & Jerry's in order to forge an alliance between business and social change. So for several months, we kept on experimenting, adding a little of this, taking away some of that, until they were satisfied—and now the chocolate fudge brownies have become a very important part of our bakery's financial health as well as its social mission.

Many people won't take a step until they think that they know what the right thing is. There is an expression, "Do the right thing." But how do we know what the right thing is? We can't know for sure. Maybe we should just say, "Do the next thing." And if we do that—whatever it is—to the best of our ability, chances are it will turn out to be the right thing as well.

15
TO PROFIT OR NOT TO PROFIT

Businesspeople are fond of talking about the bottom line. But in the long run, business, social action, and spirituality all have the same bottom line. This bottom line not only includes your financial profit, it also includes the good you are doing in the community, and the spiritual transformation of the individuals who work together.

We have to take all these areas into account—even if we think we are interested only in profits measured in dollars and cents. Any business needs people to work in it and a community to sell it. And the more involved the workers or employees are and the more prosperous the community is, the more profitable the business will be. It's just common sense. A bottom line that takes all three aspects into account will be the bottom line that maximizes profits as well.

THE PAYOFF

The payoff function is the single factor that drives a business, or any enterprise. In the for-profit business world, the payoff function is usually profits as measured in dollars and cents. In a not-for-profit enterprise, however, the payoff function might be measured by the number of people who receive meals every day, or the number of homeless people who receive shelter.

But the truth is that the bottom line, like life,

is never so simple. My mathematical graduate work was in optimization theory. Because of this, I see the bottom line consisting of both a payoff function and constraints. From the standpoint of the payoff function, we might consider these constraints as limitations, but they also force us to look for realistic solutions.

When I was at McDonnell-Douglas, for example, I worked on planning a mission to Mars. Naturally we wanted to accomplish the mission in as short a time as possible in order to save fuel and to get the astronauts back to their families as fast as possible. That was the payoff. But we also had a very important constraint. The faster you go, the hotter the temperature—and you can't raise the temperature of the craft above a certain degree without it burning up.

For the Greyston Bakery, the payoff function is money measured in profit. But there are certain constraints on that profit. One of the constraints, for example, is that the people who work in the bakery have to be paid enough to be well housed. Another constraint is that they have to have medical coverage. We also have the constraint that the bakery takes part in community development. We might also add the constraint that they have a successful family life, or that there are opportunities for spiritual growth.

In the Greyston Family Inn, which is a not-for-profit social action project, the payoff function might be measured by the number of families that have gotten off welfare. But a constraint might be the income that the Greyston Family Inn generates.

In the Zen community, the payoff function

might be the number of people who have become enlightened. But one of the constraints might be whether they are also happy! Or whether they have a good family life or are able to earn a decent livelihood, or whether they help other people.

We seem to have an unfortunate tendency to deny reality, but reality has a way of sneaking up on us. It will always win in the end. Actually, the more constraints you add, the more realities you are dealing with. And the more realities you are dealing with, the more effective your business will be. Some people worry that the more constraints you include in your bottom line, the smaller your actual payoff or profit will be. Many businesspeople had a similar concern when the notion of quality control arrived from Japan—they thought that figuring in the cost of quality control would drive profits down. But that was not the case, and now everybody includes quality control as a necessary constraint in the bottom line. In the future, I think we will have to include a kind of quality-of-life control in every bottom line. And that quality control will include things like spirituality, health, and community development.

TO PROFIT OR NOT TO PROFIT

There are two extreme views: the for-profit business view that thinks only about money, and the not-for-profit business view that thinks business is dirty. But by not including profits in their bottom line, not-for-profit social activists actually end up weaning people away from self-sufficiency. And by not including community development in the bottom line, for-profit businesspeople weaken both their own workers and their customers.

The future for both business and social welfare organizations, I feel, lies in a synergistic approach that makes use of both for-profit and not-for-profit approaches. Both for-profit and not-for-profit approaches can support and help each other.

The Greyston Bakery is a for-profit business that has the social mission of a nonprofit service organization. That mission determines its location in the inner city, its emphasis on entry-level job creation, and its strategy of not automating faster than workers can move up to higher-skilled jobs, as well as self-managing work teams and an overall environment of support, respect, and friendliness. In turn, the bakery's commitment to inner-city development has magnetized customers who share strong social values, and this has led to increased business for the bakery. Being selected by Ben & Jerry's as its sole supplier of chocolate fudge brownie chips is an outstanding example of how this works; in fact, Ben & Jerry's shifted its brownie business away from another supplier because of the "added value" represented by Greyston Bakery's social mission.

The other side of this coin is that because the bakery is a for-profit business, turning a profit is a top priority. As measured by Dun & Bradstreet's 1994 summary of production bakeries, the Greyston Bakery was in the upper 30 percent regarding both return on sales and assets. The profit motive encourages the long-term growth and survival of the organization, and this in turn keeps the social mission viable. There are many nonprofits that do job training, and do a good job of it. But they're dependent on outside funding support and consequently can be forced to downsize or go out of business in spite of their good work. Joining the approaches of a nonprofit and a for-profit business joins the virtues of social benefit with the strengths of self-sufficiency.

SELF-DIRECTED MANAGEMENT TEAMS

At the Greyston Bakery, we have begun to experiment with using self-directed management teams as a way of using economic incentives to support individual growth.

Self-directed management teams work best when they are linked to worker incentive—the more the crews produce, the more money they make.

The crews themselves take responsibility for the people they bring in. They also train the people themselves. They won't tolerate crew members who have serious problems with drugs or alcohol or absenteeism or lateness because it affects the money all crew members make. There is also a powerful incentive for the crew to work well together.

Usually, it's management who wants to install clocks and keep close track of hours. But a couple of months ago, a woman came up to Jef's office to ask for a clock down on the floor. When Jef asked why, she said, "There are a lot of people taking breaks and we want to know how long they're taking for breaks!"

Unskilled or disadvantaged workers cannot be turned into skilled and socially responsible workers overnight. For this reason, we have instituted a three-phase program.

In the first phase, workers are closely supervised. The emphasis is on developing basic workplace skills, such as showing up on time every day and getting along with coworkers and supervisors.

In the second phase, workers are organized into work teams, which take on much of the supervisory role themselves. Pay is linked to production.

In the third phase, the workers will manage the business through self-directed work teams. In this phase, the workers will own shares in the business.

Self-directed management teams may have an economic motive, but they also have far-reaching educational, psychological, and even spiritual effects. They lead to self-sufficiency and pride and teach people how to help each other and work harmoniously together toward a common goal. In addition, they can play an important part in revitalizing our inner cities by creating a well-trained, socially responsible, and autonomous workforce.

DEFINE YOUR BOTTOM LINE

The bottom-line concept has to be applied to both for-profit and not-for-profit organizations. As manager, you have to involve everyone in the discussion about what the bottom line is for your enterprise, including both your payoff function and as many constraints as you can identify. Every situation is different. You need dialogue to determine the best mixture for your company or project. That very discussion will help you set your vision and values. It will help you to clarify the true purpose of your business and your life.

COOKING A BUSINESS

In cooking a business—or any kind of organization, for that matter—we have to find a way for each part of the organization to maintain its separate integrity, its taste, while making sure that it works well with all the other ingredients.

This is quite difficult to do, because it's natural for each part to develop its own ego and move away from the others. As soon as we start weaving a net of communication, the pieces start coming apart. But we can't catch as many fish in a small net as we can in a big one, so we have to find a way to keep the pieces together.

The Jewish mystics say that at the very beginning of creation, the holy flame burst into billions and billions of sparks and that these sparks have to be brought back into the holy flame.

This means that every moment things are trying to split apart. I want to be separate from you. I want my group to be better than yours, or my division to do better than yours. I want this organization to succeed more than that one. So the tendency for sparks to fly off by themselves gives rise to the need for somebody to bring the sparks back together into the unity—the one life, the whole life, the holy flame—that they really are.

The person who brings the sparks back together is the master chef, or the Zen cook. And the holy flame is the great feast of the supreme meal.

The organizing principle—at least for the Greyston model—is the living, dynamic interplay between spirituality and livelihood.

The Greyston Bakery, for example, provides jobs for homeless families housed by the Greyston Family Inn. The Greyston Family Inn creates housing and child-care for bakery workers. Both the bakery and the Family Inn provide job training and life-skills counseling. And the Greyston Builders create both housing for Greyston Family Inn and jobs for minority construction workers who live in the building.

At the same time, we are trying to create an environment conducive to spiritual growth and transformation—not by advocating specific spiritual practices, but simply by creating an atmosphere where nonduality and the interdependency of life can be directly experienced.

We are not talking about creating a precious or self-consciously spiritual atmosphere, however. The workers in the Greyston Bakery listen to rap rather than to New Age meditation music. But self-management teams can lead to a natural concern for the whole group and to a very clear experience of interdependence. A clean, well-organized environment can strip away dualistic confusion. Training people to focus on the moment in their work, rather than on a future goal, can encourage a meditative awareness of the present. And not depending on a technological solution sometime in the future helps us find continual small improvements that can be implemented here and now. The natural consequence of such an environment is for people to seek spiritual practices or guidance appropriate to their lives.

In this way, both our daily life and work itself can become conducive to spiritual transformation.

16
SERVING AND OFFERING

In Japan, there's a practice called *takahatsu*, literally "carrying bowls," in which the monks go out every day to collect food. It dates back to the old days of the Buddha, before the monks settled down in monasteries with kitchens.

But the practice of *takahatsu* is not just about collecting food offerings. It's also about how to deal with all the offerings. The monks wear large straw hats that hide the upper half of their faces. They do not look directly at the person making offerings or at the food that is offered. Whatever is given is accepted with gratitude.

Not everybody understands or appreciates this practice. There's one story about a monk who was begging and a woman who yelled at him, "You lazy monk, go do some work!" and poured a big bucket of water over his head. The monk got upset and angry. When he returned to the monastery, his teacher reminded him that in *takahatsu* everything, good or bad, should be accepted with equanimity. The monk, said the teacher, should have accepted the women's anger as an offering.

In the same way, it's also important to learn how to deal with the various offerings we receive from life. Sometimes we might get too much, or too little. Sometimes we might be scolded or cursed. And sometimes we might receive a big offering of praise, which is often harder to deal with than all the other offerings we might receive.

MAKE YOUR HOME YOUR TEMPLE

A few years ago, the Dalai Lama, a Buddhist monk who is both the spiritual and temporal head of Tibet, met with a group of rabbis in New Jersey. The Dalai Lama asked the rabbis how the Jews had kept their religion and culture alive during the two thousand years they had been in exile from their homeland. The Tibetans had been in exile from their country for thirty years, he said, and he was concerned about the future of their religion.

One of the participants, Blu Greenberg, told the Dalai Lama that the Jews had kept their religion alive because of an ingenious thought the rabbis had after the temple was destroyed. The rabbis had said that each home should be a temple. So they ritualized the Sabbath. The candles were laid out in a certain way on the tablecloth, and the whole meal became the offering. Traditionally, the candles are lit in a certain way, then the meal begins with a ritual washing of the hands, and there's a blessing over the bread and wine, so that the Shabbat meal becomes a communion, every week. The Diaspora didn't destroy the tradition because the family carried it on. Most important, the children were also involved in it. The Dalai Lama thought that was very interesting because, he said, "When our kids come to the monastery, they usually fall asleep."

MAKE YOUR BUSINESS YOUR TEMPLE, TOO

Going to the *Zendo* or the temple or the church is a beautiful thing, but we should be careful not to fall into the trap of thinking that the temple is the only place you can practice your religion. Even though we have a *zendo* in our community, I try to make sure people understand that they can practice meditation at home. In the Catholic Church you have to go to church to take communion, which is fine. But if you're not around a church, you miss your communion.

I think the Jews made a very wise move by bringing their religion into the home. But it's not only our home that's our temple. Our work and business is also the temple. When we started the Greyston Bakery, we built a *zendo* on the top floor of the bakery, above the offices. We sanded the wood and polished the floors so we would have a place to sit in meditation at work, too.

That's a key part of what we're trying to do. When we're cooking the meal of our life, our business has to be our temple. We don't just do our business and then go somewhere else to be spiritual. Being spiritual— however we define it—is one of the basic ingredients of business.

Spirituality is also one of the basic ingredients of social action. Unless some kind of personal transformation takes place—both in the people helping and the people being helped—no fundamental change can take place. Without such transformation, we are still locked into the worldview that separates us from reality. Whatever change there is will be quantitative rather than qualitative. Fundamental change will come about only when we break the walls of our deluded views. Institutions, after all, are made up of individuals.

But we have to be very careful not to push spirituality, or anything else for that matter, on anybody.

No one at the Greyston Family Inn is asked or expected to become interested in Zen or any other religion. However, we do offer various programs dealing with issues of self-esteem and personal development, and we are supportive of spiritual involvement in any form.

In business and social action, in life itself, spiritual transformation is the yeast that makes the bread rise.

FOOD FOR THE BUDDHAS

In the Zen monastery, when the cook finishes cooking, he bows toward the assembly of monks waiting in the meditation hall for their meal and offers a portion of the food to the Buddha, to the cooking fire, to the guardian deities of the kitchen, and to the hungry spirits. Then he greets the head server, who offers food to the monks accompanied by the sound of a dramatic drumroll.

Because eating is not seen as a time for relaxation but as a continuation of meditation, the monks eat sitting on their meditation cushions in the meditation hall. Before they eat, the monks recite a chant enumerating the seventy-two labors that went into making the food—the farmers who turned the soil and planted the rice, the people who picked and threshed it, on up to their fellow monks who are serving them as they chant—reminding themselves to live in such a way as to be worthy of all the effort that has gone into this meal.

The monks eat out of special bowls modeled on the begging bowls used by the Buddha, called *oryoki.* The *oryoki* bowl is the container of just the right amount of food. The right amount of food is different for everybody because everybody requires a different amount of food. There's no such thing as a little or a lot. The monks eat exactly what they need, no more or less. They signal with hand gestures how much food the server should put into their bowls. They can ask for seconds or even thirds. But they have to be careful not to ask for too much, because leftovers are not allowed.

MAKE IT LOOK GOOD

In the West we have a very different way of serving food, of course. But the principle is not really so different. When we take the care to arrange food in a pleasing way on platters, and when we take the care to set the table, we are also making a kind of offering.

Even though we might say we are eating because we are hungry, we don't eat right from the pot in the kitchen, nor do we just take the ladle and slosh food out soup-kitchen style. We wait, with a certain amount of patience and even renunciation, for the food to be arranged and presented properly. The presentation of the food and the arrangement of the dishes, candles, and flowers on the table are a very important preparation for eating.

When we eat food, we're nourishing ourselves and satisfying our hunger. But the proper presentation of food also feeds the sense of sight and beauty and color and proportion.

In our social work, I always include aesthetics as part of what we're doing. Most social workers don't do it that way. When they see the care we take with the aesthetic aspects, they say, "What's that got to do with their bellies or their jobs?"

The answer is, it has a great deal to do with the people we're serving. People need housing and food and jobs, but people are not just housing and food and jobs. They're much, much more. Human beings always have an aesthetic dimension. Beautiful surroundings inspire people to live more fully and to appreciate the preciousness of our world and each other. The beauty of art and nature also reminds us of the inner harmony and splendor that is every human being's birthright. The Japanese understand this very well. Every house or noodle shop, no matter how humble, contains a *tokonomo*—a niche to hang a painted scroll and exhibit a small flower arrangement. It's a small thing, but it uplifts the spirit and adds dignity and grace to everyday life.

Art also plays an important part in empowering people. Mitch Snyder, the founder of an innovative shelter and community in Washington, D.C., found that programs in theater, painting, and writing were tremendously effective in helping homeless people get hold of their lives again.

Maybe the aesthetic aspect of serving is generally lacking in our society because the cooks are not looking at their guests closely enough. Maybe they're feeding their own image of a homeless person.

I've never understood a soup kitchen to be just a place where you throw food around. It seems to me a soup kitchen should be a restaurant with tablecloths and flowers. It should be a place of dignity. That's because when I look at those I'm serving, I don't see lepers, I don't see abstractions like "the homeless." There are no statistics on the street. All I see are people, who appreciate the same things I do. So I may not have the money to do everything in the way I want to do it. But with the ingredients I have I can certainly do the best job possible. The aesthetic aspect of things is reflected in the very structure of our building. We have a pale blue awning covering the sidewalk outside the building at 68 Warburton. In the backyard, we're building a secret garden for kids, a fairy-tale kind of place, with a waterfall, a climbing tree, and shrubs to play hide-and-seek in. It's fascinating to me how many people will walk through the building and say, "This doesn't look like housing for the homeless," just because we're creating permanent housing that's a pleasure to live in and has some dignity. In one sense they're right. The building isn't housing for the homeless, because there are no homeless people living there. They all have apartments, and some are working toward ownership. The situation is continually changing. There's a whole new set of ingredients to work with now.

Aesthetics is also very important in business. (Some businesspeople make the mistake of thinking that's *all* there is.) In the bakery, for example, the appearance of the pastry is a very important element. It's part of cooking to learn how to put icing on the cake. It's actually just like doing calligraphy. The icing gun is the calligraphy brush, and the icing is the ink. The decorations on the cake not only make it look beautiful, but the line also communicates something of the spirit that went into baking the cake.

FROM HELL TO HEAVEN

There is an ancient Zen scroll that shows heaven and hell. In hell, the hungry ghosts are all sitting at a great banquet table filled with all kinds of delicacies, trying to feed themselves with very long spoons. But no matter how hard they try, they cannot reach their mouths.

In heaven, the hungry ghosts are sitting around the same banquet table. But these hungry spirits are feeding each other with their long spoons, so that they all can eat.

This is the way to transform our world from a hell to a heaven. Only when we offer a portion of our food to our fellow hungry ghosts can we satisfy our own deepest hunger.

OFFERING GOES TWO WAYS

After we have recognized and appreciated all the labors that brought us this offering, we offer some of it back.

If we don't offer something back to the community when we create a business, we're only taking from the community. And if we don't offer something back to the planet, we're only taking from the planet. It's just like farming. If we don't rotate the soil or fertilize it, eventually the soil won't support us.

So in a meal we give an offering back. Just picture it—if you don't give it back, all those hungry ghosts will come back and grab all your food. If you just let people get poorer and poorer, the situation will deteriorate and eventually explode

So the Zen cook always gives an offering back—to the hungry ghosts, the community, and the earth itself. And then we realize that what we're eating is an offering as well. We're always serving and receiving—it goes both ways.

17
HOW TO EAT

Eating is the culmination of everything we have described—the cleaning and preparation, the gathering of ingredients, the cutting and chopping and mixing with various tools, the cooking, and the serving. Eating is the climax. It's the ceremony of feasting or communion or receiving blessings or giving thanks.

We should eat in a way that expresses our appreciation of our food and all the effort that went into making it. We should savor the tastes and the texture of our food. In order to do this, it's good to eat slowly—or at least slower than we usually do. And we need to pay attention to what we are eating, as well as to the people sharing our meal. We should take our time. Some people recommend chewing rice fifty times before swallowing it. That might be going a little too far, but at least we should chew our food well so that we can savor the six flavors: the bitter, sour, sweet, salty, mild, and hot.

When we eat with this kind of awareness, we will find ourselves eating just the right amount, whatever that is for us, like the Zen monks in the *oryoki* ceremony. Undereating is related to a lack of appreciation for the ingredients, the cook, and the server—for our whole lives, in fact. Overeating is related to not wanting the meal to end, or to hanging on to the enjoyable sensation of eating. But too much of anything, even a good thing, soon becomes painful. It's like wanting to hold on to wealth and profits in business. When that happens, the flow stops and the result is constipation, which rots you from within.

LIFE AND DEATH

Eating also expresses the paradoxical nature of life itself. When we eat a meal we have cooked, we find that everything we have created—all our work—has been for consumption, for annihilation. Life is a constant process of creation and destruction. We can't hold on to the meal we've made. We have to use it. In fact, when we eat our meal thoroughly, with appreciation, we find there's nothing to hold on to.

Food is both an offering and a sacrifice. In the Zen tradition the first precept is nonkilling. One way we study the first precept of nonkilling is to consider all the beings that have given up their lives for our lives to continue. At each moment, this life is being created and clothed out of billions of offerings and sacrifices. So the first precept becomes a tremendous appreciation for the flow of life.

As our experience of life increases and deepens, we spontaneously minimize the amount of sacrifice needed for our sustenance and begin to live more simply. An intensified gratitude for this infinite support system moves us to make the best possible use of all that sacrifice. For example, we might become vegetarians rather than meat eaters. Although eating meat and eating vegetables both involve taking life, we might feel a difference between eating things that are conscious of being killed and things that are not.

The powerful irony at the heart of Zen practice is that the strongest way to follow the first precept of nonkilling is by "killing the self." If we can kill—that is, truly forget—the self, we are at that moment nurturing and fostering life in the fullest and most genuine manner possible. When we kill the self, we eliminate the separation that threatens life and makes killing possible in the first place, because *zazen* is being there for the wholeness of life, not just for the pieces we like or don't like. It means not experiencing separation, not seeing the other person as different from me.

Recently I thought of the Buddha's life and I thought of his father trying to isolate him from suffering, from old age and death. That became a metaphor for the denial or separation from those aspects of ourselves or society that we are afraid of or not ready to deal with. In the last five to ten years I've felt a need to bear witness to those aspects of society that I fear or deny.

For me the importance of bearing witness to what is denied grew out of my *zazen*, out of bearing witness to life as a whole. When I bear witness, I learn, I open to what is. There is a healing process in that. And the things that we are in denial about teach us. We don't go to them to teach them. They teach us.

LEAVE A LITTLE SPACE

Yasutani Roshi used to say that the first two-thirds of our meal is for ourselves and the last third for the doctor. He meant it's unhealthy to fill ourselves completely. It's better to leave a little space. We don't want to overtax our systems.

Air is food also, and breathing is a kind of eating. In Zen meditation, we think of the belly as a balloon.

When we breathe in, we don't fill the balloon to the breaking point. We leave a little space. And when we breathe out, we don't let the balloon deflate all the way. Because we want our breathing to be continuous, we leave a little air in to make a smooth transition.

The same rule applies to business. If the bank is willing to loan you five hundred thousand dollars, think about taking only four hundred thousand. If your business is expanding very fast, like a balloon, consider cutting the growth rate down by 20 percent or so. Let it grow, but leave yourself some breathing room.

DAILY BREAD

Because we eat two, three, or four times every day, it's easy to forget how wondrous that is. It's like the sunrise or the sunset. The sun rises and sets every day. If it's an especially beautiful sunrise, we may notice it. But if it's not "special," we may not even see it.

But if we can see it as if for the first time, each sunrise becomes very special and very beautiful. And so with each meal we create.

In Japan, people bow to one another all the time. Zen students bow to their teacher, of course, but we also have a tradition of bowing to the teacher even when the teacher's not there. In fact, we say it is more important to bow to the teacher when he's not there.

In the same way, I think, it's important to celebrate even when we might think there's nothing to celebrate. It's important to have a feast when there's nothing to have a feast for.

When we were still working on the building,

we put a Christmas tree up on the roof and decorated it with lights. Even though the building wasn't finished yet, we took that time to celebrate.

It's easy to bow to the teacher when he or she is there. It's easy to celebrate when there's something to celebrate for. But it's more difficult and more important to see the potential of life all the time, to create every meal as if it were the first and last meal we've ever eaten.

When we offer and serve this supreme meal, we don't just feed people or even teach them how to cook—we teach and inspire them to teach and inspire other people to teach and inspire other people how to cook. If you cook only for yourself, you will never be satisfied, no matter how much you eat.

So when you offer the supreme meal, it becomes an endless chain reaction of instructions to the cook. Dogen says that every teacher should have at least one and a half successors—at least one and a half students who can pass on what they have learned. If you can teach more than one person to cook in that way, then your teaching will eventually permeate the whole universe.

There is a koan about a monk who comes to the Zen master Joshu and says, "Please give me a practice."

And Joshu says, "Have you eaten your meal?" Which means, in Zen talk, "Have you tasted enlightenment?"

The monk says, "Yes, I have eaten a meal."

"Good," Joshu says. "Then go wash your bowls."

Joshu's "wash your bowls" was pointing out that enlightenment should not leave a trace. But he was also pointing out that it is very difficult, if not impossible, to eliminate all the traces. It's like the tortoise in another Zen story. The tortoise always leaves footprints on the sand. And then the tortoise's tail wipes away the footprints. But then the tortoise's tail leaves tailprints!

So it's almost impossible to eliminate all our traces. We may eat all our food, clean the counters, wash the dishes, and scrub the pots. But then we have to wipe the soap off the counters, and clean the sinks, and then we find ourselves left with dirty sponges, and as we look back, we notice that we've tracked some of the dirty water on the clean kitchen floor.

In the same way, as we drop the conditioning or attitude that keeps us separated from the next thing, that very process creates a certain amount of conditioning, and then *that* has to be dropped away, too.

Joshu's "wash your bowls" is about this process. Even though it may not be possible, we should try to leave no trace of what we've done. Therefore we don't walk around saying, "I've been enlightened," or "I've made this great product." If our enlightenment is genuine, it will express itself in the way we act in ordinary life.

In the Zen monastery, after the monks have eaten everything that's in their bowls, they clean the bowls with tea or plain hot water. Then they drink the water. The water that's left over in the bowls goes back into the gardens.

This traceless "nothing left over" has a very profound spiritual meaning, but it also has a very practical ecological application. If there's any trace left over, it should be used again—and again until nothing is left over. If you're a manufacturer you have to take into account what happens to a product after it's used up. You have to think about how your product will go away. Whether you create a new car, a new refrigerator, or a new cookie tin, you have to create a way for your creation to be recycled.

If you do that, if you get rid of the traces of the car you've built, or of the wonderful banquet you've just eaten, you open up the space so that you can see a whole new set of ingredients. So eliminating the traces is really another way of saying we're cleaning up, which is where we began.

Leaving no trace is what Zen calls "nonduality." Subject and object collapse. The distinction between the helper and those who are being helped disappears, as does the distinction between giver and gift, or cook and guest.

Actually, Dogen doesn't suggest that we cook our whole meal and then clean up at the end. He tells us that no trace should happen *as* we're doing it—so that nobody knows what we've done.

So we clean up while we're cooking. We eliminate traces as we go. And yet at the end there's still a stage of cleaning up, just as there is at the beginning. Although we've created that stage of no-trace, although we're going to start all over—we still start with cleaning up, even if we walk in and everything looks clean already. Even though we may feel very calm, in a deep state of concentration, the way of the Zen cook is to always start with a little centering and return to Beginner's Mind so that we can clean up and take stock of our ingredients.

And now we're ready to begin again.

19
STARTING AGAIN

When we finish something, whether it's a meal or a project, our whole world has been destroyed. But that annihilation or consumption is obviously not the end of our work or our lives. Only when we have finished something have we created the space to make something new.

Of course, this is another way of saying that nothing is ever really finished. No single meal—no matter how delicious or how nutritious—will put an end to our cooking and eating. In Buddhism, the bodhisattva makes a vow not to enter nirvana in order to enjoy his or her own enlightenment until *all* sentient beings have attained enlightenment. Since new beings are born every second, this will obviously take a very long time, possibly forever.

So the bodhisattva's work, like a mother's work, is never done. In the same way, a master chef is always cooking the next meal, whether it's the supreme meal of emptiness that frees us from hunger, or the very basic solid meal of the soup kitchen. What matters is that we keep on living our lives to the fullest, savoring the meals we cook, offering our food to all the hungry spirits we invite into our kitchens.

Many people are shocked to hear that I've already begun applying for funds to renovate more buildings. It shocks me to think that they're shocked. They seem to think that we did this so that we could hold on to the building we have. But you can't hold on to a meal you cook. You have to serve it, eat it, clean up, and go on.

By "finishing" this project, we have a model that can be replicated. But we don't necessarily have to worry about whether or how it will provide a model for other people in other places. If it's a healthy model, they will adapt it to their own situation.

If we look at the building now, with all the traces of rebuilding and moving cleaned up, we find that the ingredients are completely different from three years ago, when the families were living in motels and the kids were being bussed to schools. Now the families are living in their own building, and we have lots of new ingredients. And so we have a whole new meal to cook. It won't look anything like it did over the last three years, when we took a deserted building and renovated it so that we could take families living in motels scattered around the county and give them a permanent place to live.

But if you looked at the tenants of the building in the same way you were looking at them a few years ago when they were living in motels, you'd be seeing the wrong ingredients.

We are actually preparing two different meals now. One meal will result in the self-sufficiency of eighteen families. The other will result in the families living together in the building so that this building will become a model for other buildings. Just down the block, for example, there's another apartment building with people living in it who are not talking to one another or not doing anything to help their community. So our building, Greyston Inn, can possibly become a beacon for community development.

Of course, timing is always important. You always cook for yourself first, as we said. So before they can go out and help anybody else, they have to work to develop their own self-sufficiency. But even now they can go back to the motels and tell their friends that there is a way out of the pattern of homelessness.

That's the twelfth step of the AA model of fellowship, which is very close to the bodhisattva's vow. In both cases, you vow to help other people. The inhabitants of Greyston Inn might take a vow not to stop until no one is homeless. In any case, helping others is the best way to make sure you don't slip back yourself.

The end result of the bodhisattva vow is that it empowers the guests to become cooks themselves. This is true for all of us. When we realize that we cook the meal of our lives, then we can become master chefs. When we do this, we find ourselves where we have always been—in our homes, in the marketplace, in the kitchen. We may see the world differently, but we continue to do what we have always done. In the end, we become what we have always been.

So you've got to clean the table and start all over. But now you start from a new state. Because after you eat, everything has been transformed. Life has been transformed into life. It doesn't do any good for the ingredients to stay in the cupboard or for the books to stay on the shelf. The facility we've prepared, the apartment building, has to be lived in. The furniture has to be moved in—which will scratch the freshly painted walls. It's just like a new car that has to be driven in order to suffer that first scratch. Then you can drive without worrying about what might happen.

Things have to be used. We have to *live* our lives. The meal should be eaten and digested completely. In fact, we should live and use ourselves so thoroughly that it's impossible to know that the activity happened. When we really do something completely, nothing is left.

Dogen has a famous statement: "To study the self is to forget the self. To forget the self is to be enlightened by all things. . . . And this traceless enlightenment continues on forever."

THE THIRD VOW

I had forgotten all about my vow to live on the streets of the Bowery until I had been working with the homeless for about a year. Then it came back to me. And once that happened, I knew it was something I had to do.

Of course I had no idea of how to accomplish this. It was another experiment. We did have a little help, though. Dean Morton of the Cathedral of St. John the Divine had directed an urban ministry program in Chicago during the sixties. Ministers and social workers who studied there had to spend a few days experiencing what the street was like. They called it "Taking the Plunge."

Dean Morton arranged for us to speak with him and a few formerly homeless people who worked with a church group. He advised us to stay open to the unexpected. The homeless folks gave us mostly useful information, suggesting places where we could sleep and missions where we could eat. They warned us to stay away from the big city shelters, since people got robbed, raped, and knifed there, and AIDS as well as a drug-resistant form of tuberculosis were rampant. They also warned us to keep our shoes on while we slept so that they wouldn't "walk away."

We started asking for help, as people on the

street do all the time, weeks before the retreat began. I had asked the people who planned to go on the retreat to raise money for each day they were on the street, which meant that far more people were involved in the retreat than those who actually took part in it. Some of this money we contributed to organizations working with the homeless, including the missions where we ate, and some was used as seed money for a new project that would provide housing for homeless people with AIDS. As it turned out, we raised more than thirty thousand dollars.

Normally when we go on a retreat we go to a place in the country, far away from the problems of life that we're trying to deal with. We go to a place where we let the issues that are bombarding us settle down so that we have a clear space—an empty mind—from which to look at those issues. We might also go on a retreat to get together with friends or coworkers to work through difficulties, brainstorm, or plan the future.

Our approach on the street retreat was a little different. It was a retreat *into* the problems we were working with. The Zen cook learns more from the situation than from a study of the situation. It's like the difference between reading about something and actually tasting it. We wanted to taste and experience the ingredients of homelessness directly and then let the solutions arise directly from those ingredients. We felt that if we did a retreat in which we became street people, there would be a good chance that we would learn something that would help us work with the problems of street people.

The same principle could be applied to business. Let's say there's a problem between labor and management. We could go away and meet with our peers and discuss the issues and conflicts in production, or in keeping the bakery or office clean. And then we could come back to the plant and try out our solutions.

But we could also create a retreat that would take place right in the plant. We could shift roles. We could live the other person's role so that we experienced life from another perspective. If you were a manager, you might become a worker or employee. And if you were an employee, you might become a manager.

We might not like the experience of the taste, but at least we'd know in our bones what the problems were. When we experience things in this way, we begin to live in the unknown instead of living through our concepts. And when we do that we have a much better chance of figuring out how to use and transform the things we don't like to make a wonderful meal.

We began our street retreat with ten dollars, which meant two dollars a day, and the clothes we wore. The men were instructed to let their beards grow for a couple of days. Each person carried only his or her social security card for identification. I had made up a schedule, and we agreed to meet three times a day to do *zazen* together and talk about what was happening to us. But the very first day we found out it didn't work, because my schedule said we were going to sit at seven, and it turned out the soup kitchens were open at seven. Then we found out there just wasn't enough time to get together three times a day, although all we were doing was finding places to eat, to pee and shit, and to sleep. If you're walking from place to place—it also rained the whole week—surviving takes up all your time. So we were right down to the basics. But we did find time to meet for *zazen* twice a day in a "crack park" down in the Bowery.

I didn't know what to expect, but the retreat turned out to be one of the most profound in my life. I would say that at least 90 percent of the twenty-one people who did the retreat—and it didn't seem to matter if they did it full-time or for just a few days—had deeper experiences than in almost any retreat I'd seen anyone go through.

None of us really wound up suffering. We were not experiencing homelessness. We all knew we were going back home after four days. But we were experiencing living in an environment that forced us to forget about all the other aspects of life and made us deal directly with eating, sleeping, and surviving. One night we slept in boxes we found on the street. It was cold, the pavement was hard, the streetlights were shining, and there was noise all night. The street stripped us bare.

We ate mostly in missions and soup kitchens. We sat through gospel services. Though many of us didn't like the idea that people were more or less required to do this in order to eat, it was also true that people were receiving real food for the soul. They were hearing that Jesus loved them just as they were. We met a number of people who had been transformed and saved—both literally and spiritually—by the food the mission had offered them. I realized even more strongly than before that food needs to be both for the belly and the spirit.

We also experienced a certain amount of rejection. People seemed afraid of us. They didn't like the sight of us, or the smell of us. As soon as they saw us, they would turn and look away. People who would normally have shown us some respect, like storekeepers, didn't want us in their place.

Our retreat ended with a Passover service and an Easter Mass, because Easter and Passover happened to come together that year. We held the services in the open, in the park in front of City Hall. As we began, a number of homeless people appeared out of the night, drifting into the park to join us for these sacred meals.

Rabbi Don Singer spoke about how Passover commemorated the passage of the Jews through the desert out of captivity to freedom. We passed out matzoh, which is the simplest kind of bread possible—just water and flour with no yeast—to everyone. The bread is unleavened because the Jews had no time to let it rise as they tried to escape. But he also said that the unleavened matzoh had another, spiritual meaning. It was to remind us not to be "puffed up" with ego, and not to be arrogant.

Then Father Kennedy celebrated Mass. He held up the host—which is also the simplest kind of bread, a wafer made of just bread and water—and said it was the body of Christ, and he offered grape juice as the blood. And he quoted Isaiah, saying that you can't be whole until you've first been broken.

After we finished our spiritual meal, we served a small feast. The Greyston Bakery truck brought boxes of Rain Forest Chocolate Chip Cookies. And we served soup, which we had been eating all week, except that our soup was matzoh ball soup. It was strange, in a way, to be standing suddenly on the other side of the line, the tables turned, serving instead of being served, but I think we could do it a little better, a little less puffed up, more like a matzoh than a cheesecake you might say, because we had stood on line in the rain ourselves, even if only for a few days.

The next morning, in our basement *zendo*, we chanted the chant that offers the supreme meal to all the hungry spirits. I realized I had fulfilled the three vows I had made so casually in a pizza parlor thirty years before. But of course I also thought about how much more needed to be done.

And so I found myself renewing my vow. Maybe it would take forever to feed and house all the hungry ghosts in all the worlds. But however long it took, I thought, I would do my best to keep on cooking and serving the most delicious and joyous feast I could.

ABOUT THE AUTHORS

Bernard Tetsugen Glassman is abbot of the Zen Community of New York and also the Zen Center of Los Angeles. He is founder of the Greyston Mandala, a network of businesses and not-for-profits doing community development work in southwest Yonkers, New York. Drawing on its Buddhist roots, Greyston's approach integrates the economic, social, educational, and spiritual dimensions of each endeavor.

Roshi Glassman is a former aerospace engineer who worked on manned missions to Mars at McDonnell-Douglas during the 1970s. He holds a Ph.D. in Applied Mathematics from UCLA. He trained in Zen Buddhism under Taizan Maezumi Roshi in Los Angeles. Roshi Glassman currently serves as president of the Soto Zen Buddhist Association, spiritual leader of the White Plum Sangha, cochair of the Board of the Temple of Understanding in New York City, and as a director of the Social Venture Network, the AIDS National Interfaith Network, and the Community Planning Council of Yonkers.

Rick Fields is the author of *How the Swans Came to the Lake: A Narrative History of Buddhism in America* and *The Code of the Warrior* and editor of an anthology, *The Awakened Warrior*. He is the co-author of *Chop Wood, Carry Water: A Guide to Spiritual Fulfillment in Everyday Life* and cotranslator of *The Turquoise Bee: Love Songs of the Sixth Dalai Lama*. He is a contributing editor of *Tricycle: The Buddhist Review* and editor-in-chief of *Yoga Journal*. He lives in Berkeley, California.

David A. Cooper
Silence, Simplicity, and Solitude
A Guide for Spiritual Retreat
Required reading for anyone contemplating a retreat.
0-517-88186-1 Softcover

Marc David
Nourishing Wisdom
A Mind/Body Approach to Nutrition and Well-Being
A book that advocates awareness in eating.
0-517-88129-2 Softcover

Kat Duff
The Alchemy of Illness
A luminous inquiry into the function and purpose
of illness.
0-517-88097-0 Softcover

Noela N. Evans
Meditations for the Passages and Celebrations of Life
A Book of Vigils
Articulating the often unspoken emotions experienced
at such times as birth, death, and marriage.
0-517-59341-6 Hardcover
0-517-88299-X Softcover

Burghild Nina Holzer
A Walk Between Heaven and Earth
A Personal Journal on Writing and the Creative Process
How keeping a journal focuses and expands
our awareness of ourselves and everything that touches
our lives.
0-517-88096-2 Softcover

Greg Johanson and Ron Kurtz
Grace Unfolding
Psychotherapy in the Spirit of the Tao-te ching
The interaction of client and therapist illuminated
through the gentle power and wisdom of Lao Tsu's
ancient classic.
0-517-88130-6 Softcover

Selected by Marcia and Jack Kelly
One Hundred Graces
Mealtime Blessings
A collection of graces from many traditions, inscribed
in calligraphy reminiscent of the manuscripts of
medieval Europe.
0-517-58567-7 Hardcover
0-517-88230-2 Softcover

Jack and Marcia Kelly
Sanctuaries
*A Guide to Lodgings in Monasteries, Abbeys, and
Retreats of the United States*
For those in search of renewal and a little peace;
described by the *New York Times* as "the *Michelin
Guide* of the retreat set."
THE NORTHEAST *0-517-57727-5*
THE WEST COAST & SOUTHWEST *0-517-88007-5*
Softcover

Barbara Lachman
The Journal of Hildegard of Bingen
A year in the life of the twelfth-century German saint—
the diary she never had the time to write herself.
0-517-59169-3 Hardcover
0-517-88390-2 Softcover

Katharine Le Mée
Chant
*The Origins, Form, Practice, and Healing Power of
Gregorian Chant*
The ways in which this ancient liturgy can nourish us
and transform our lives.
0-517-70037-9 Hardcover

Gunilla Norris
Becoming Bread
Meditations on Loving and Transformation
A book linking the food of the spirit—love—
with the food of the body—bread.
0-517-59168-5 Hardcover

Gunilla Norris
Being Home
A Book of Meditations
An exquisite modern book of hours, a celebration
of mindfulness
in everyday activities.
0-517-58159-0 Hardcover

Gunilla Norris

Journeying in Place

Reflections from a Country Garden

Another classic book of meditations

illuminating the sacredness of daily experience.

0-517-59762-4 Hardcover

Gunilla Norris

Sharing Silence

Meditation Practice and Mindful Living

A book describing the essential conditions for meditating

in a group or on one's own.

0-517-59506-0 Hardcover

Ram Dass and Mirabai Bush

Compassion in Action

Setting Out on the Path of Service

Heartfelt encouragement and advice for those ready

to commit time and energy to relieving suffering

in the world.

0-517-88500-X Softcover

His Holiness Shantanand Saraswati

The Man Who Wanted to Meet God

Myths and Stories that Explain the Inexplicable

The teaching stories of one of India's greatest

living saints.

0-517-88520-4 Softcover

Rabbi Rami M. Shapiro
Wisdom of the Jewish Sages
A Modern Reading of Pirke Avot
A third-century treasury of maxims on justice, integrity,
and virtue—Judaism's principal ethical scripture.
0-517-79966-9 Hardcover

Ed. Richard Whelan
Self-Reliance
*The Wisdom of Ralph Waldo Emerson as Inspiration
for Daily Living*
A distillation of Emerson's spiritual writings for
contemporary readers.
0-517-58512-X Softcover

*Bell Tower books are for sale at your local bookstore or
you may call Random House at 1-800-793-BOOK to
order with a credit card.*

If, after reading this book, you would like to learn more about Greyston or help in its work, you may write to the following address:

Greyston Foundation
21 Park Avenue
Yonkers, NY 10702